THRILLS OF THE NORTHERN TRAWL

by

Skipper Albert Hutchinson
("Hurricane Hutch")

Commanding Steam Trawler "*Arsenal*"

Written at Sea

First published in Great Britain in 1938
by
Hutchinson Publishing

This edition published 2008 by Adeson Publishing

Copyright © 2008 Adeson Publishing

Names, characters and related indicia are copyright and trademark
Copyright © 2008 Adeson Publishing

A CIP Catalogue of this book is available from the British Library

ISBN 978-0-9558361-0-7

Printed and bound in
Great Britain by Biddles Ltd,
King's Lynn, Norfolk

This book owes so much to my gaffer, Sir John Marsden, Bart., Chairman of the Consolidated Fisheries Ltd.; to Mr. R. Jackson, O.B.E., Secretary of the British Trawlers' Federation, Ltd.; and to Captain Allan K. Taylor, a Fleet Street Journalist, that the convention of thanking these gentlemen is not only a pleasure but a duty.

Albert Hutchinson
Grimsby
April, 1938.

CONTENTS

INTRODUCTION

How many of us, accustomed to the well-filled slabs in the fishmonger's shops, and to that tasty morsel on our dining-tables, realize that men must literally face death and maiming in a thousand terrifying forms before the ocean's harvest can be brought to market?

That this is no mere colourful exaggeration will be appreciated if we are reminded that the town of Grimsby alone lost no fewer than eight trawlers with all hands to a total of 63 lives only three seasons ago, in the winter of 1935.

Daily these sturdy little vessels prance down the broad waters of the Humber, proud, defiant, in single file, double file, treble file, dozens of them, scores of them, hundreds of them, outward bound for the North Sea, the Faroes, Bear Island, the white Sea, the Murmansk Coast, manned by the men of The Northern Trawl, the finest seamen in the world.... British Fishermen.

Not so long ago this was the same breed who swept the deadly, hidden mine from the Ocean Highways; these the gallant little vessels that cluttered in convoy round the merchantmen, like young whales round the mother fish, easy fodder for torpedoes, and welcome, as long as the big sister reached safe anchorage with food for the women and children of England, and stores for our fighting forces, their intrepid, daring, and unselfish sacrifice inspiring the poet to write: 'Ships of Iron, and Men of Steel…Gentlemen Unafraid !'

But these men are always at war, and in regions and seas which spew death in far more countless and fearsome ways than all the lethal weapons ever devised by the devilry of man.

As far as eighty North they force their puny craft, in fog and ice-pack, in blizzard and hurricane, towing all alone in the winter darkness of the Arctic night, sailing almost to within the shadow of the Pole in their insatiable quest, and eternal sacking of the desolate Northern Seas.

Well are they named "Men of Steel," for only a cold, savage courage, superhuman endurance, and a dogged determination might enable human beings to defy the mighty elements, and triumph over the incredible odds which our fishermen must face during every winter voyage.

Their story has never been told, and who better fitted to tell it than a man who has sailed the Northern Seas for the better part of half a century? For just that length of time the author of this thrilling epic of the seas, Skipper Albert Hutchinson, has been trawling the Northern Seas.

Known to all fishermen as "Hurricane Hutch," he is recognized as the crack Skipper of the Iceland Seas, and the story of his exploits, contained in the cover of this book, forms one of the most amazing narratives of sea adventure ever hitherto published.

Simply told, rich in the inimitable expression of his calling, absorbing in its human appeal, it grips the imagination and holds the interest from the time he sails down the Humber, where the story begins, until he rings down the curtain, and steams through the lock-pits of Grimsby Docks, homeward bound.

"In over thirty-one years at sea," writes Skipper Hutchinson, "I have spent less than four years ashore, mostly in spells lasting on an average thirty-six hours a-tween trips. That's the price my wife and kids have had to pay for fish."

The rough notes of this epic story were actually prepared in the Skipper's log at sea, and another passage runs "This Iceland coast, off which I am fishing now, stretches for 2,000 unbroken miles. We call it 'The Graveyard.' In winter, for eight long months, that treacherous surf-line, littered with 'blinders,' is hidden either by thick, impenetrable fog, or blizzard, or the eternal darkness of the Arctic night, and wind-swept, during most of the period, by the devastating fury of North Atlantic gales, or the full force of a tidal swell which strikes the fear of God into the stoutest hearts.

"In winter it never lets up. No, it never lets up, and pitted here and there along this cursed coast, for it is accursed, you will see, if you look close enough, the gaunt skeleton remains of what were once little trawlers . . . fitting tombstones indeed for those of my pals who have gone a-fishing."

The Saga of the Northern Trawl! But we will leave Skipper Hutchinson to tell the rest of this stirring story in his own inimitable style and language, untouched by any other pen.

ALLAN K. TAYLOR,
Editor.
Fleet Street,

FOREWORD

BY

SIR JOHN MARSDEN, BT.

Chairman of the Consolidated Fisheries, Ltd.
Britain's Largest Fishing Fleet.

London, E.C.4. March 1938.
"Ye gentlemen of England who live at home at ease
Ah! Little do you think upon the dangers of the seas"

S o runs the old song that many of you have heard and it is strange to consider how true it is to-day, island race though we be. We have one of the most important fishing industries in the world; it is our sixth largest industry, yet except in the case of people living at the ports, how little is understood about it by most of us! We are so accustomed, as we are reminded at the beginning of this book, to the well-filled slabs in the fishmongers' shops and the piles of golden fried fish in the fish friers' that we rarely give a thought to the risks that are undergone or the labours that are expended in order that we may be offered day in, day out, our choice of prime fresh fish.

Today, when we are urged to produce as much of our food as we possibly can, our fishing industry is more important to us than ever. It is an asset of which we may well be proud. The trawlers that bring the harvest of the seas to us are built in British shipyards. They are equipped with British gear and stores, bunkered with British coal and manned by the finest seafaring race in the world - British fishermen.

In this thrilling story of Skipper Hutchinson's adventures he describes the life, very fully, of our fishermen who scour the seas in the Arctic waters in order to keep us supplied all the year round with fresh deep-sea fish. But I think it will add to the general interest, and help readers to better follow the narrative, if I prepare a somewhat lengthy explanation of the early history of this great fishing industry of ours, and further explain how it is carried on at the present time.

The art of fishing is one of the oldest in the world, yet to this day the fisherman is simply a hunter - the last of the hunters we may call him - who must still take his life in his hands and face the perils of the seas, and is in direct descent from the primitive men who depended solely on their skill with trap and spear for their daily food.

Very little is known about the early development of fishing as an industry in this country, but we do at least know that the earliest ventures were confined to rivers, lakes, and estuaries. It was obviously impossible for the ancient Briton in his coracle to venture far from land.

As early as the third century A.D. fish was caught in considerable quantities round our coast. Far back in the fourteenth and fifteenth centuries we find that a great deal of fresh fish was eaten in those districts that were near enough to the coast to obtain it by packhorses, and that there was a brisk trade in salt fish to other parts of the country.

In those days it was not possible to keep cattle alive during the winter as there were no winter crops of turnips, mangel-wurzel, or seed-cake, such as we have to-day, and therefore it was necessary to kill off the cattle in the autumn and salt down the meat for winter consumption.

The monotony of a diet of salt meat was very great, and even salt fish made a welcome change, while fresh fish was considered a wonderful treat.

That is why we rind it so often chronicled that presents of fresh fish were made to important personages and received with the utmost graciousness.

The rise of the fishing industry really began in 1347, when a Dutchman invented an improved method of curing herrings, a method which is followed in all essential points to this day. The Dutch were quick to push home the advantage which this discovery gave them, and by the end of the fifteenth century we find that the Dutch fishing industry was supreme in Europe. So greatly did their shipping increase as a direct result of their trade in salted herrings that they became the chief naval European Power, whilst the English sea power fell sadly into decay.

In Queen Elizabeth's time the condition of English shipping was so bad that serious consideration was given to the best ways of helping the fishing industry. It was suggested that instead of one 'fast-day' a week, two should be observed - Wednesday and Friday.

In the library of the Society of Antiquaries in Burlington House, London, there is a quaint old broadsheet preserved that was issued in 1593. This broadsheet, or leaflet, quotes a statute of queen Elizabeth's reign, in which dire penalties were threatened for those who did not observe the 'fish daies'.

It was evidently issued to help the fisheries, or, as it said, "that fishermen (the chiefest source for mariners) might the more be increased and maintained". The broadsheet is decorated with a finely drawn sailing ship and fishermen in a small rowing boat, and certainly has a very attractive appearance.

Thus, our fishing industry continued in a far from flourishing condition until the early part of the nineteenth century, although various attempts were made to establish it. One method tried was the granting of bounties to fishermen as rewards for good catches of various fish, especially herrings.

But naval wars and the depredations of press gangs continually reduced the number of our fishermen, right up to the peace of 1815. The industry progressed rapidly from that year, and in 1829 was so well established that all bounties were withdrawn.

We can take 1829 therefore as one of the most important dates in the history of the industry. From that time it steadily developed both in value and extent.

Fleets of sailing smacks and drifters sprang up all round our coast, manned by a magnificent race of men, sturdy and independent, courageous and skilful. A sailboat was generally the property of a group of fishermen, very often of one family. One of the group, called the ship's husband, remained on shore to dispose of the catch and buy new stores and tackle as required. The others worked the boat and fished, and the proceeds were divided amongst the members of the group. Every harbour round our coast, little or big, possessed these communally-owned sailing boats, and great was the pride in them of their owners.

These sailing smacks are disappearing fast, and that is unfortunate, for they were, indeed, things of beauty, although, of course, the limitations of these small craft were very great. Very often they were prevented from going to sea by rough weather; then, again, lack of wind made it impossible for them to trawl. Again, the area in which they could fish was naturally a very restricted one. They had no space for stowing and icing the fish. It would, in fact, have been impossible for them to have supplied the whole nation with fresh fish each day as our great fleet of steam trawlers does nowadays.

Then came steam, and with the introduction of steam fishing vessels about 1880 a totally different state of affairs began in the fishing industry.

Not only were the new vessels able to go much farther afield than the sailing smacks and fish in practically all weathers, but they were able, owing to the use of steam winches, to handle far larger nets and fish in deeper waters.

In the organization of the industry also radical changes took place. It proved impossible for many of the small groups or families of fishing folk to join together and buy a steam trawler, for apart from the great expense of such a vessel, they can only be handled in large and specially equipped harbours, where all facilities are provided for the unloading and dispatching of huge quantities of fish. Thus, from the first, trawlers were owned by large limited companies instead of by individuals, and the industry has become centralized in ports such as Grimsby, Hull, Fleetwood, Aberdeen, Lowestoft, Swansea, and a hundred smaller ports.

Since the first steam trawling company was formed in 1882, with a fleet of four vessels which fished on the Dogger Bank, the British fishing industry has gone ahead by leaps and bounds.

Last year British fishing vessels landed over 21½ million cwts. of fish with a value of over £15,000,000.

Today our fishing industry is divided into two principal sections-trawling and drifting. The fish that live in deep waters are caught by trawlers. They are called 'demersal', or deep-sea fish. Herrings, pilchards, and mackerel, which are called 'pelagic', or surface-swimming fish, are caught by drifters, which wait for the shoals of these fish to appear off our coasts. In this story, Skipper Hutchinson is going to tell you about the deep-sea or trawling industry, which provides about 85 per cent of the fish which is eaten in this country.

The coming of steam trawlers had a serious effect upon the little fishing communities round our coast. Unable to compete in the deep-sea industry, many of those fishing villages have suffered severely. It must be remembered that their type of fishing, 'inshore' fishing it is called, could never catch enough fish to supply the whole nation with one of its most valuable foods, as our deep-sea industry does.

It is one more illustration of how the introduction of machinery and the scientific application of it causes hardships in the transition stages, but at the same time is the means of enormous benefit to the nation at large.

Yet a curious thing is that in nine cases out of ten when our fishing industry is mentioned landsmen's thoughts turn at once to this inshore fishing, which to-day produces not one per cent of the fish we eat, and the main industry with all its ramifications is practically unknown. Probably this is due to the fact that when on holidays at the seaside these little fishing craft are seen and vividly remembered, whilst very few of us come into contact with the deep-sea industry.

At the present time there are about 1,800 British trawlers, and they not only scour the North Sea and all the seas round our coasts, but they also make long journeys to the Faroe Islands or to the Icelandic fishing grounds, or right within the Arctic Circle to Bear Island, or even to the White Sea and Murmansk Coast of Russia. Some even make voyages to Greenland, over 2,600 miles away. These far northerly grounds are becoming more and more important to us, for every year a greater proportion of our deep-sea fish comes from these Arctic regions.

Grimsby and Hull, our two largest fishing ports, send out most trawlers for these tremendous voyages. Aberdeen, our third largest fishing port, does not usually fish so far afield. Fleetwood, our fourth fishing port, renowned for its hake, fishes mostly off the north coast of Ireland, the west coast of Scotland, and in the North Atlantic grounds. Milford Haven, and other South Wales ports, which also catch a great deal of hake, fish off the south and west of Ireland, and sometimes still further south off the coast of Morocco.

The North Sea is still the most important of our fishing grounds, but it is fished so intensively by so many nations that our trawlers have had to find out all these new distant grounds in order to keep us supplied with fish. Even in the old sailing days there was much good-humoured rivalry in the North Sea. The Yarmouth men would call the Hull men 'Yorkies', the Hull men retorted with the nickname 'Norfolk dumplings', Lowestoft men were termed 'Peabellies' on account of their supposed fondness for dried peas. The men from Barking were known as 'Duffies', and so on. Foreign fishermen were also given names. The term 'Scrub' includes foreigners of all nationalities.

As a joke, this was all right, but when fishermen began to have serious quarrels the different governments concerned had to step in. About fifty years ago meetings were held to agree on the rules for North Sea fishing, just as you have rules for football. Now each nation has fishery gunboats to act, as it were, as referees.

A steam trawler may not be a handsome-looking vessel, but she has the distinction of being probably the most seaworthy craft afloat. She must be low in the water, for one thing, as it would otherwise be impossible to bring the heavy bags of fish on board, but Skipper Hutchinson explains this very fully. Trawlers will carry on with their fishing through wild winter weather, with the waves sweeping the Decks and the men continually wet to the waist, in spite of their thick thigh boots. Needless to say, they are always ready to go to the aid of another vessel in distress and have never been known to refuse an appeal for help on the high seas. In the War, our trawlermen swept the seas clear of mines for us and earned the title of 'Gentlemen Unafraid'. It is a title to which they have just as much right today, for they show the most superb courage, daring, and endurance in their daily work.

A modern steam trawler is built of steel and is about 150 to 170 feet long with a gross tonnage of from 400 to 550 tons. It costs as much as £28,000 to build and put to sea! And the engines, particularly, must be very powerful, for speed is one of the great factors in fishing today - speed to get to the fishing grounds and, above all, speed to get back to port when the fish-hold is full. Moreover, there is an enormous strain on the engine when it is dragging a heavy bag of fish along the sea-bed.

Long-distance trawlers require as much as 260 tons of coal per voyage, and, in addition, 70 tons of ice for storing the fish are also carried.

The crew of these modern vessels is normally nineteen hands - skipper, mate, bo'sun, cook, chief and second engineers, two firemen, and eight deck hand, two spare hands, and wireless operator.

The newest ships are equipped with wireless for communication with their home ports, direction-finding gear for finding their position by wireless signals from special wireless stations, and echo-sounding apparatus which tells them the depths of the sea. In some, the fishermen can even have a hot bath, an unheard-of luxury until recently.

Each trawler is provided with several trawl nets. These nets are huge, conical-shaped bags of netting roughly 100 to 120 feet long, with a span of from 90 to 120 feet at the mouth, and a depth at the mouth when trawling of from four feet six to six feet. When trawling, the net is dragged slowly along the sea-bottom, scooping up all the fish that comes in its way. Skipper Hutchinson will tell you that other things, sometimes gruesome, are caught in that net occasionally.

On the way to the fishing grounds these nets are carefully overhauled and got into order. Meanwhile, the skipper or 'Old Man' as he is called, whether he is an old sea-dog or a youngster of twenty-two or twenty-three, has set the course for the fishing ground where he thinks he will find most fish. It is the skipper's responsibility to find the fish - he decides where to go and if he fails he gets no wages, for both skipper and mate are paid a percentage of the ship's takings. The rest of the crew have a fixed wage. As fish are very elusive creatures, the skipper must have a first-rate knowledge of their habits.

Thus, he must know at which seasons of the year they are most likely to be found on certain grounds.

You must remember that it is only possible to fish in the shallower parts - or Continental shelves - of the ocean. But it is possible nowadays to fish as deep as 350 fathoms, although most fishing is carried out in much shallower water, say from 70 to 250 fathoms. Most of the Atlantic is therefore unfishable.

When the skipper has reached his chosen spot, the vessel is stopped. A cast of the deep-sea sounding lead is taken to ascertain the nature of the sea-bottom and the depth of the water, so that the fishing gear may be properly regulated. A buoy, or dann as it is called, bearing a flag by day and a lantern by night, is lowered into the water to mark the centre of the trawling operations.

All hands are called on deck to assist in casting the net into the sea - or 'shooting the trawl' as it is called. The trawl net is attached to the ship by two powerful ropes or warps, which are wound on to steam winches. When the order to shoot the trawl is given, the steel warps are run off the winch.

Usually it is necessary to run off a length which is three times the depth of the water in which trawling is to take place.

The warps are taken around the various bollards on deck and shackled to the two trawl boards to which each side of the mouth of the net is attached. These trawl boards or doors, as they are usually called, are heavy wooden constructions, about 10 feet long by 5 feet wide, and are shod with iron. They weigh 15 cwt. apiece, and constitute what is called the 'otter' trawl.

The function of these boards is very important. You know how the wind pulling against a kite keeps it straining in the air. In the same way, when the trawler pulls the warps through the water, the boards are so arranged that the pressure of the water on them keeps the mouth of the net open.

In rough weather, with the sea sweeping the decks, the rolling and pitching of the vessel makes the lowering and hauling of these heavy boards exceedingly dangerous and the men have to be on the alert to avoid serious injuries.

Generally the fore trawl board is slung overboard first and hangs over the side suspended from the 'gallows', a bow-shaped device to which the 'door' is attached.

Next the net itself is thrown overboard, and last of all the aft-board is slung over. The engines are then put full speed ahead, and when the trawling gear has drifted well aft of the vessel, the correct length of warp is paid out. By carefully watching the warps a skipper can tell how they are entering the water and if the trawl is working efficiently or not.

Meanwhile the vessel steers slowly ahead, towing the gear over the bed of the ocean at a speed of 2½ to 3 miles per hour for an hour or more.

Attached to the upper edge of the mouth of the net is the headline - a cable of, say, 100 feet in length - along which are strung floats which are either thick glass globes in bags of net or hollow metal balls.

The duty of these floats is to keep the headline up when the gear is being towed along the sea-bottom like an open purse.

To the lower edge of the net is fastened a heavy manilla rope - the foot-rope - which by sweeping along the ground helps to make the fish rise into the net. When trawling on rough ground large wooden rollers or 'bobbins' are attached to the foot-rope.

In the net itself pockets are formed in the sides so that fish reaching the narrow end, or 'cod-end', as it is called, and trying to return, usually enter the pockets. Also a flap of netting is suspended some distance inside the mouth of the net. It is easily lifted by incoming fish but the pressure of water on it tends to prevent their escape.

When the skipper gives the order, 'Time to haul', all hands are called on deck. The trawler is stopped and steam winches are put into action to wind up the warps. And now a strange thing happens.

At the first sound of the steam winch - no matter how far from land - hundreds of sea-gulls make their appearance out of the blue. The winch is their dinner-bell, and they make haste to be in time for the hauling in of the bag.

In they come flocking, circling, and wheeling. Mingled with the noise of the winch you hear the fluttering of hundreds of wings and the screaming of the kittiwakes, of grey-backs and herring-gulls, and often of solan geese and gannets.

The winch continues to wind in. The trawler is carefully manoeuvred into the 'weather position' so that whatever wind there is will blow her away from the gear, not on top of it. It may take ten minutes to haul in the otter-boards, which are at last hung up again in the gallows. Next the head-rope is hauled on board.

Slowly the net is brought nearer the trawler. The rising up of the bag is eagerly awaited. The fish are now all congregated in the extreme end of the net-the cod-end. As the net nears the surface the pressure of the water is lessened, the bladders of the fish become distended, and - if it is a big bag - the whole bag is suddenly buoyant and comes to the surface with a rush.

When a foot or so below the surface of the water, the white sheen of fish in the meshes of the net can be seen, the excitement amongst the birds is intense, and they make slanting dives at lightning speed into the water, emerging with wriggling fish in their beaks.

It is not only the birds that watch for the uprising of the net. All eyes on deck are fixed on the bag, anxiously hoping for a good haul, and great is the skipper's satisfaction if it comes up with a rush.

The winch has now come to an end of its hauling and the last part of the work must be done by hand.

The crew grasp the net as it comes alongside, heaving in inch by inch, helped by the roll of the skip when she rolls towards the net and holding fast as she rolls back.

A rope is next passed round the cod-end. One end of this rope is attached to a wire rope leading to a block near the top of the mast. This tackle is worked by a winch, which finally lifts the bag, probably containing a ton or more of fish, until it is swinging over the deck.

Seizing the right moment, one of the men crouches beneath it and catching hold of the 'cod-rope', a specially tied rope holding together the cod-end, he gives it a pull, and out pour the silver, shimmering fish into one of the wooden enclosures, or 'pounds', as they are called, on the deck.

The opening of a big bag of fish is a truly remarkable sight, especially at night under the glare of the electric lights. A tumbling mass of fish falls into the pounds. With them come shellfish and all sorts of beautifully coloured seaweeds, as well as crabs and other sea creatures.

For the moment the fish are disregarded - the gear has to be shot again. If the net is undamaged, it is put over the side again, immediately. If it is torn, the second trawl is brought into use until repairs can be effected.

Once more the cod-end is put overboard, followed by the rest of the gear, the doors are shackled on again and lowered into the sea. The ship is again manoeuvred so that the mouth of the net is extended by the doors, the skipper gives the order 'Steam ahead', and all is made shipshape for another three or four hours' trawl.

Now the cleaning and gutting of the fish is started. The crew turn to with knives, and the viscera of the fish are thrown to the screaming gulls, except for the roes of certain fish and the livers, which are retained for the manufacture of oil. This done, the fish are sorted into baskets according to species and size, are washed well, and then lowered into the fish room, where they are stowed away in ice.

It is bitter work in the pounds in winter weather. The men are exposed to all the fury of the elements.

They are nearly frozen by the icy blasts and almost invariably soaked through by the breaking waves.

Yet they are known to carry on even when they have to be lashed to the mast for fear of being washed overboard.

There is little rest, indeed, for the men once fishing operations have begun. Work goes on unceasingly, day and night, until the hold is full. Every now and again the order to 'Haul the trawl' is given, and the whole operation is repeated.

The most the men can hope for are snatches of rest between the time when the cleansing of one haul of fish is finished and the next haul. After several days and nights of this strenuous work, small wonder that they are all nearly exhausted and much too tired for their usual chaff and banter.

Meanwhile the cook has not been idle. Good food and plenty of it is the universal rule in a trawler, and just as important as the food are the mugs of scalding tea that are always 'on tap'. No matter what the hour of the day or night, the kettle is ready. Gallons of tea are drunk daily ; it is the trawlerman's only beverage, and it is said truthfully that a tax on tea affects fishermen more than any other section of the community.

Fish figures largely on the menu, and you may be surprised to learn that fishermen never seem to tire of eating fish, or of singing its praises as a food. When you think of the strength required for their strenuous lives, you realize how splendid a diet it is. In addition, what are known as 'cookings of meat' with plenty of fresh vegetables are prepared for them, and boiled dumpling, or 'duff', as they call it, follows. Many ships keep up the custom of adding currants and raisins to the duff on Sundays, when it is called 'plum duff'.

The gutting and cleaning and stowing away of the fish are in the direct charge of the mate, and the value of the catch when it reaches port depends very largely on his vigilance. Badly cleaned fish make very much less money than those which are carefully handled.

It may surprise you to know that there are over thirty kinds of deep-sea fish landed daily from our trawlers, and all of them are excellent eating. Some day, perhaps, we shall, as a nation, learn to value our sea-larder as it deserves to be valued and use it far more frequently. At present very few people use more than, say, half-a-dozen fish and, strange to say, it is the cheaper and more economical fish that are too often neglected. Hotels and restaurants make full use of these lesser-known fish, and it is a pity that housewives do not also appreciate this supply of cheap food that is waiting for them.

For instance, sea-bream is a delicious fish that is very much prized in France - but too rarely met with in a fishmonger's shop here. France buys most of her supply of this fish from us, and then when English people cross the Channel they say, "What lovely fish they have in France," and do not realize that they could have it here for the asking.

There is another fish, the gurnard, that has a very white sweet flesh, and is eaten in some parts of the North of England, but is quite unknown elsewhere.

Another fish that is considered a great delicacy by fish connoisseurs is the John Dory, found off the South Coast, and a strange shape he is, but he is beautifully coloured and looks very handsome flashing through the water. French people call him St. Peter's fish, because of the round spot he carries, which they say is the mark of St. Peter's thumb.

Then there is the dogfish, which is a ferocious fish and is apt to scare away the other fish from the fishing ground. They often do great damage when caught in the trawl, taking huge bites out of the other fish and sometimes damaging the nets badly. But when skinned and properly prepared for the table they make very good eating. In the South they are known as 'huss' and they have a number of other local names, including 'Sweet William'.

But the most familiar fish of all is the cod. This is the most important of all our fish, for far and away more cod is caught than any other deep-sea fish. Last year cod formed 35 per cent of our total catch of deep-sea fish, haddock came next with 25 per cent, hake next with 6 per cent, plaice fourth with about 5 per cent, and all the other twenty-six or -seven kinds made up the remaining 29 per cent. So you will see how important cod is. It is easy to know cod when you see it by the barbel or 'beard' on its chin.

Of course, as already mentioned, the trawl net often brings up strange creatures, and some of them are very destructive to the nets. Often a shark is hauled aboard. Often, too, very curious objects are caught in the trawl. Tusks and bones of mammoths which once roamed where now the ocean rolls are by no means uncommon.

Old anchors, portions of lost cargo, a bale of goods, a barrel of wine may appear with the fish in the cod-end. They may cause the crew long hours of labour mending the nets.

All landsmen think of a ship lost at sea as something gone forever. To a fisherman every 'total loss' raises visions of a 'fastening' round which, sooner or later, some unlucky skipper will wrap a trawl. A skipper must know the bed of his fishing ground as a farmer knows his fields, and must calculate just where to sweep his trawl so as to avoid the hidden obstructions.

And now to return to our trawler. When the fish-hold is full and the last haul has been made, the dann buoy is lifted, and everything is made shipshape for the run to port. Now, at last, the men can have the rest they have earned so well, and right glad they are to turn in. Back races the trawler to its home port, and now comes the important question, "How much will our fish make?"

Early each weekday morning whilst you are probably still in bed, the trawlers take their places at the quayside and the fish are quickly unloaded and laid out for sale in rows, the last caught always in the first row.

Next comes the auction, at which the fish is sold to the highest bidders. Then there is a scene of tremendous activity as the fish are rushed away, packed in ice in wooden boxes, and despatched by special fish trains throughout the length and breadth of the land. No other country in the world has such a splendid distribution of fish, and other nations envy us because our fish is so fresh and so plentiful.

I have told you how some of our trawlers fish right up to the Arctic ice. In mid-winter these voyages are veritable polar expeditions. The men must contend with blinding snowstorms and dreaded ice-fogs. Freezing gales load the deck and rigging with frozen spray and thus bring the added peril of overwhelming the vessel by the sheer weight of ice.

Yet, in spite of all hardships, the fisherman loves his life and rarely indeed casts eyes of longing at the landsmen's existence. He would not exchange the freedom of the great ocean, the thrill that comes after fighting through a storm, the triumph of bringing home a catch snatched from the icy jaws of wintry seas for a life within four walls.

When at night we hear the wind howling round our chimneys whilst we are sitting cosily round the fire, we should remember the fishing fleet afloat on the dark, stormy seas. We should remember, too, all that the fishermen have done to protect us in the past, and resolve to do both ourselves and them a good turn from now on by eating more of the harvest of the seas which they gather in for us.

A last word about Skipper Hutchinson, and this story - a story, I might add, which is true and accurate in all its amazing detail. Hutchinson is a bluff, bighearted fisherman, typical of his breed, who has crowded his years with stark adventure, risking life and limb, week in, week out, for fish and daily bread.

To understand just all that means, and the price men like "Hurricane Hutch" have to pay-well, read his story. I will vouch that it will both thrill and enthrall you, and make you gasp in places.

JOHN MARSDEN.
Chairman,
Consolidated Fisheries, Ltd.,
Fish Docks,
Grimsby.

THRILLS OF THE
NORTHERN TRAWL

Chapter 1

THE GAMBLE

Aboard S.T. Arsenal.
Trawling Lat. 62° 15" N. Long 41° 20" W.
S.E. Coast of Iceland.

"Nowt doin', lad. No, nowt doin'!" That's what I said to my 'gaffer', Sir John Marsden, when he asked me to write this yarn. Then he started to talk, an' I listened, an' fell. He said the story had never been told, said everybody ate fish but knew very little about them, or how they were caught, as we catch them, in millions, said the wimmen folk would be interested, especially about the different kinds, the quality and the price.

Well, I know lots of wimmen who know all about the price. They've paid to the full, God knows, and not in pounds, shillings, and pence either. However, I'll have something to say about that later on, maybe.

"What language would you expect me to write it in?" I asked the old 'gaffer', when he'd finished his crack.

That took the wind out of his sails for a second.

"Why, English, of course, Skipper," said he, cocking his eyebrows.

English! Holy blazes! Aye, and jumpin' hell

"I don't know it, Gaffer," I told him. "The only language I know is fisherman's language; you ought to know that."

Aye, that's the only lingo I know-fishermen's language-every second word a curse, an oath, the one an' only safety valve that helps us to keep our manhood and self-respect when Old Feathery Legs is doin' his stuff.

Aye, Old Feathery, curse him! The Black Devil who rides on every crested wave north of 65°. He and his Hell's Legions, the fog, the blizzard, the black-squall and the hurricane…' Blow, damn you!

Howl, blast you !'…An' we raise our puny fists and curse him, just to try an' kid him, an' ourselves, that we're not afraid.

Aye, that's why we trawlermen curse, loud an' often, but I reckon it's mostly bluff. It's either swear or slobber, sometimes. I've seen strong men slobber like kids down North come winter time.

I've seen our lads up to their waists in water on the foredeck, guttin' fish in th' pounds, a black-squall screaming around, an' the temperature 40° below zero. I've seen them fast asleep on their feet, reeling like drunken men, their brains numb…dead …working like automatons, aye, an' they've been on that deck for thirty…forty…fifty hours, grafting like fiends an' never a break or blink of sleep a-tween. I've seen a wave, high as the mast-heads, crash on deck and sweep all hands in a heap in the lee-scuppers, seen their arms an' hands clawing up through the boiling surf, still graspin' wriggling fish an' guttin' knives, an' from the bridge I've looked down and counted the bobbin' heads…one…two…three… four…not once, but twice, aye, thrice over, to see if all were aboard. An' all too often there's one fine young lad missing. We see his white face for a second, the eyes, wide-open, staring, pleading, and then he's gone… gone…an' never a murmur, never so much as a squeak.

Reckon that's the only time we bless a cold so intense sometimes that I've seen it freeze a sleeping man's eyelids together as tight as an oyster shell.

Death in these winter seas is quick and merciful, thank God… Instantaneous!

Exaggeration ! Is it? I've seen the weather so bad we've had to lash men to the mast so's the work might go on, as it must go on, blow hard, blow low, incessantly…eternally.

Aye, I reckon it comes natural to swear sometimes, although Johnny-the-One at the Post Office doesn't think so. Perhaps if he reads this yarn he'll see our point of view. It's a sore point with us. He's got policemen sitting along the North Sea coastline wiggin' to our chat, on Trawler wave-length 100-140 metres. Some of us have been hauled before the courts and fined £10, but Old Feathery, the black weather devil's the one he wants, not us. We don't ask anyone to tune-in when we're yarning over the radio-telephone. Them that does might remember that that wave-length is there for our benefit, paid for by our gaffers (owners) to help us to catch fish, aye, and sometimes to save life.

All our latest ships now carry a receiving and transmitting radio-telephone installation. The one on my vessel, the *Arsenal*, cost £2,000, and from as far North as 80°, almost within sight of the Pole, I've spoken to pals up Humber way.

We cannot cross-talk, like an ordinary telephone. Our present gear only allows of a one-way speech.

That comes in useful sometimes. We can tell the other fellow to go to hell and then switch off. When we want him to answer we use the words:

'Over to you', or simply 'over', then we listen to what he's got to say.

We'll hear a big spate of messages blaring out of my loud-speaker, which is just at the back of me here on the bridge, before this trip's finished. Some will raise a laugh, perhaps, but there are others!...

Aye, there are others!

"Mayday! Mayday! Mayday!" That's the trawler's SOS, derived from the French M'aide - 'aid me', and one night not long ago, when the *Jeria* went down with all hands off Stalberg Corner, not far from where I'm fishing today, this is the message which came throbbing out of that sinister black box behind me. It came from young Skipper Bill Emsley, a pal of mine.

"*Jeria* calling all trawlers!...He's got us...Old Feathery's got us at last!...We can see the rocks now...just astern!...Another minute, I reckon!...We're on!...Good-bye, pals...Say good-bye to my wife...to my kiddies...Good-bye, Grimsby!...Good-bye, Eng...!"

These were the actual words, spoken calmly, almost coldly, without a trace of emotion. His brother was listening-in on another ship, and nearly all of us had relations aboard the stricken vessel. The last word of that message was never completed.

"Good-bye, Eng...!"

Then silence. Only the silence!

Some say we abuse this radio gadget, use it to discuss domestic matters, sex, horse-racing, football, and other things. Being human, maybe we do sometimes, but believe me for twenty-three hours every day it is used entirely for the job on hand.

If you doubt my word, tune-in 100-140 between midnight and six in the morning, that's the best time, any day of the week, Sundays included, but take my tip and don't, unless you've got your ma-in-law or any pals in the house you want to be shot of in a hurry.

"Between midnight and six in the morning, Sundays included," I hear some lad repeat.

Aye, an' Christmas Day as well, lad. Twenty-four hours a day, seven days a week, three hundred and sixty-five days a year, with an extra day come a leap year, blow fair or foul, blow hard or low, them's our hours.

In thirty-one years of sea I've spent less than four years ashore, mostly in spells lasting on an average thirty-six hours a-tween trips...that's the price my wife and kids have had to pay for fish.

That's why I've agreed to write this yarn, for my pals, for our wimmen-folk. I've often wanted to see it in print, and it's about time the public learnt just how lousy this job can be.

It is lousy!

But we're not the only chaps concerned, although we number nearly

100,000 men at sea. Ship-builders, rope, net, and box manufacturers; fish-fryers, buyers (curse them), retailers, and salesmen; railways and road transport; coal, salt, and ice industries; -all these and a lot more are directly interested, and I reckon about 3,000,000 folk would have to look elsewhere for their- bread and butter if there were no trawlermen…or fish. We mustn't forget the tail-waggers.

For my pal's sake, then, an' the wimmen-folk! All right, I'll do it for them, and I'll write most about them. But we trawlermen are plain folk, remember. We've few words at our tongue-tips, if you take away the language we use when Old Feathery Legs is doing his stuff. So don't be offended if I slip in a damn, or a blast occasionally. But I won't forget this yarn'll maybe read on the Sabbath day. No, I won't forget that, for at heart we are just as God-fearing as the best, and if we do use terrible language sometimes, we never blaspheme.

No, we never curse God, no matter how hard it blows. But we pray sometimes. Aye, we do that, silently and half-ashamed maybe, but often, when He ranges the awful might of His terrible elements against us we ask that the wind may cease, an' back home, where fisher-folk gather we know there are others on bended knees.

Maybe that helps. I think He must hear them sometimes. He does, or most of us 'ud never come back.

No, we'd never come back!

But let's get crackin'! That's what we say when the trawls are ready for shootin'.

Ready!

"Stand by, all hands!"

Down below the lads are standing ranged along the starboard scuppers, backs bent, hands clawing the net, long as the ship, wide as a street, keyed to high-tension point, every muscle tense and taut, fired with the gambler's lust of make or break, 'fish fever', for this whole life is one long, incessant, savage gamble, pitted against a mighty foe who deals out death from a thousand different packs.

"Shooto!" Splash!…over she goes…the money-bag, the lucky-bag, the swag-bag! Will it come up filled with loot, or will it come up empty?

Aye, one long gamble, I think you'll agree before this yarn concludes.

I'm writing the rough notes of this log on the bridge of the *Arsenal* between hauls, so if my yarn gets a bit disjointed in places, or comes fast, don't forget we're on a ship a little less than 150 feet long, the same number of tons nett weight, with her beam, her width, a little less than 30 feet, and writing on this little lady wants some doing.

Measure her distance off in your back garden, then remember that the rails have to be low in the water to allow our heavy bags of fish to be swung aboard, and that we never run for shelter unless we're being blown literally off the face of the waters.

My crew number eighteen hands all told, including that 'Orphan of the Storm', Sparks, my Wireless Operator.

This 'Highbury Lass' dances and prances in a flat calm. In a storm she does everything but turn upside down, but no finer sea-boat sails the Northern waters, even if she does get all fussy and crusty when there's no tail-waggers around.

At the present moment we're fishing off the south-east coast of Iceland, with the East Horns, a famous landmark, about five miles off our port quarter. All along this coast the great, barren, sullen mountains eternally snow-crested and shaped like monstrous, crouching animals, sweep down to the water-line, and many a brave ship lies under the lowering, evil shadows of these terrible rocks. A grand spectacle for some, maybe, but to we fishermen they are just mountains, and the further we can keep away from the blighters the better we like it. Yow!

That's Icelandic for 'yes', about the only word I know, that and 'skoll' . . . good health.

The weather's fine and clear, by way of a change, and I'm towing with my starboard trawl astern, working a dann buoy. Now all our gadgets and expressions will have to be explained before we get crackin' properly, otherwise you'll never get the hang of this yarn. So don't get impatient to begin. I'll promise you a kick, an' plenty afore we sail much further north.

The dan buoy, or 'blister', as we call it, is actually a flag-pole kept upright in the water by a huge cork float, and secured to the ocean bottom by a cable anchor. It is lit at night by an electric lamp which burns continuously for forty-eight hours.

The blister can be seen over a distance of five miles in fair visibility, and without it some of us would come back with our fish-pounds half empty. When I come to explain the mystery of what we trawlermen call 'fish movement', and believe me, it is a mystery which may affect everybody that eats fish by-and-by, we will discover that the old blister is a very essential part of our gear indeed.

We carry two trawls, both port and starboard, although we can only fish with one at a time. The reason for that'll also come clear by-and-by.

The crew, otherwise known as deckies, brats, and a few other names beginning with the capital 'B' are busy on deck preparing the port net, just in case we come fast and spilt the starboard net on a rock or a piece of wreckage down below.

When that happens, and it happens sometimes a dozen times a day, the Skipper generally 'eats' a couple of deckies.

Sometimes we lose the whole of our damned gear to the value of £300, and never a fish in the bloody hold. When that happens the Old Man (that's me) gets his door down properly...curses the ship, damns the crew, the weather, the gaffers, all his pals, and others (especially the others), over the mike; and always finishes up by blasting the P.M.G. No offence, Mr. Postmaster-General, it's mostly bluff, as I've said afore; but, believe me, it helps.

Aye, it helps . . . blast you

Gaze round these waters from the height of my bridge. Two-thirds of the English fish harvest are plundered from these jealous seas. Some thirty other trawlers are towing in line, to lee, and windward of me, and far away on the horizon there are other smoke stacks, hundreds of them.

The Northern Trawl is here in force.

Every country on the Nor'western sea-board of Europe is represented, as well as a few from France and Spain. We're all pals at heart, and even if we do curse the 'scrub' (the foreigner) sometimes, there's only one thing matters when that message 'Mayday! Mayday!' comes flashing over the air.

Aye, country or creed makes no difference when Old Feathery's doing his stuff. No difference!

Close under the lee of the land I can see the 'bogey-man', the Iceland gun-boat, hugging the three-mile limit line, with his ugly black snout - blast him - slewed in a line with my dan buoy. I know the waters are teeming with fish inside that line, but International Law says I must not touch it, and dare I shove my stem an inch beyond he'll pounce like a famished bear. We'll leave bogey-man where he is for the present, blast him again, but we'll meet him soon, with his teeth bared-barking.

That reminds me...I want all you shore folk to understand that every word I write will be read and discussed by thousands of my pals over the 'air' from the Humber to Bear Island (75° North), and if I dare write one single word out of place, if I dare exaggerate -'spout muck!' we call that - the lads'll give me a helofa time. My loud-speaker is always turned on, just behind my left ear on the bridge, and I imagine I hear them already.

Listen in:

"*Arsenal*! *Arsenal*!...all trawlers calling the *Arsenal*! Hey, Highbury, Alex James, George Allison!

Hey, you big, fat, jumped-up son of a crab-merchant, what d'you call that damned muck you've written in that lousy book of yours? 'Thrills of the Northern Trawl' - Oh, hell! What d'you mean by it, huh?

Over to you, an' get crackin'!...Over !"

Aye, my life won't be worth a darned sprag (cod) unless I keep my weather eye lifting on this writing business.

But let's get crackin'.

I must catch about 1,500 tons of fish every year before I can wrest a living from the seas, and every year sees us going further and further North, until soon we'll be sweeping alongside the Pole itself, for that's where the darned tail-waggers all seem to be making.

The best brains in the country have been employed for years trying to solve this mysterious 'fish movement,' and if you folk at home will appreciate that there isn't enough fish caught in the North Sea, or around the British coastline, to feed London even, I think you'll agree that both the solution, and remedy, if any, affects every man, woman, and child in England. Yow!

The experts blame our trawl, so let's have a skite at our gear afore we dip the swag-bag into the pond.

We can fish to a maximum depth of 350 fathoms (2,100 feet), and as our nets must always be on the bottom, the gear must be heavy to get down that distance…and don't the brats know it.

Try and imagine what one of our trawls looks like as it sweeps the ocean bottom. Picture a huge, conical-shaped net bag roughly 100 to 120 feet long, with a span at the gaping mouth 90 to 120 feet wide, and six feet deep. In other words that bag is as long and wide as a street and above the normal height of a man. The nets are weighted at the bottom with twenty great ponderous round steel bobbins, each about thirty times the circumference of a football, threaded on a steel rope. If you can imagine a gigantic string of beads being dragged over the ocean bed with the net floating above, the great mouth kept open by two wooden doors, the upper lip of the net kept up and open in the water by several score of round tin floats, the latter the exact size of footballs, this will give a fair conception of what our swag-bags look like to the little tail-waggers below. The huge bobbins are supposed to roll over rocks and wreckage, and over the sunken valleys and dales, and thus save the net from coming fast on rocks and wreckage which litter the ocean bed. Sometimes they do, and sometimes they don't, as you will read later on. Yow!

The trawl is attached to the ship by two powerful steel ropes or warps, which are wound on to steam winches. These are threaded around the various bollards on deck, and shackled to the two doors, to which each side of the mouth of the net is fastened by hemp ropes, or head-lines.

Both these doors, about 10 feet long by 5 feet wide, and iron-shod, weigh about a ton apiece, and kill on an average ten men each year. When the ship pulls the warps through the water, the boards are so arranged that the pressure keeps the mouth of the net open, and the force of water against these doors is so tremendous that it reduces the normal speed of the ship by two-thirds. The steel warps which drag the great net astern are 3½ inches thick, with a breaking strain of 38 tons to the square inch, and it is usual to run off a length three times the depth of the water. Thus, if we are towing in the maximum depth of 350 fathoms, there is 6,300 feet of steel rope stretched behind our stern.

When that gear comes fast and these steel warps break adrift, as they sometimes do, and the Skipper fails to stop his ship instantly, men's lives are forfeit.

That chance is always present, that's why my eyes very seldom wander from these warps when we're towing, and by-and-by we'll see what happens when one snaps with a roar like crashing thunder, and flashes, curling, lashing, snake-like, through the air with the speed of forked lightning.

Those that think they know better than we fishermen say that our heavy gear, trailing on the bottom, destroys both the feeding grounds and spawn, and that the meshes of our nets should be larger to allow the smaller and younger fish to escape. If the experts are right, then of course we ought to adopt lighter gear and do away with the steel bobbins at least during the breeding season, between June and August.

But almost in the same breath, the knowing ones tell us that:

A Turbot carries	14,000,000	eggs.
A Cod carries	9,000,000	eggs.
A Haddock carries	6,000,000	eggs.
A Herring carries	70,000	eggs

These are amazing figures, but we are prepared to accept them because the late Mr. O. T. Olsen, of Grimsby, a name remembered almost in reverence where fishermen foregather, and a gentleman who devoted a lifetime to this study, has placed it on record that he once found 47,000,000 eggs in a female cod.

Now, if the scientists stand by their own figures, then we trawlermen claim that, even if we trebled, and quadrupled, the number of trawlers working the Iceland, Bear Island, and White Sea grounds, and used bobbins as big as the dome of St. Paul's, we might sweep the seas 'til the crack of doom and only murder a small percentage of the myriad billions of fish which we feel are still sheltering in the ocean deeps. No, there's another explanation.

I personally believe that some uncanny instinct is warning the fish to crowd further and further North, away from the sinister, greedy maw of our insatiable trawl. That's my belief, but even if they go to the North Pole itself, aye, and down the other side, we'll go after them. Aye, we'll go after them.

That's our job!

Fish are nearly as hard as wimmen to understand and just as contrary, at least I tell the wife that. Sometimes they like the water cold, sometimes hot, and often they're on the top making faces at our harmless trawl below, but always they're on the move.

I've fished the Iceland waters for over thirty-one years, and I'm supposed to know this lousy, heaving ditch as a farmyard duck knows its local pond. At least I've wrapped net around every blasted rock that sticks up from the rough bottom of these cursed waters. They are accursed!

But do I know them? Why, only yesterday I caught 100 baskets, 800 stone of fish, after one hour's tow in the very spot where I am now. Down went my dan buoy to mark the ground, and I blared a triumphant cock-a-doodle-do on my whistle just to annoy the lurking bogey-man hovering near by.

Then I got busy on the 'phone and tipped-off a few of my pals in code: gave them my position. A little later, over the horizon came the smoke-stacks...*Sheffield Wednesday, Spurs, Stoke City, Leicester City...* rolling their sleeves up, eager for the kick-off. We all towed for two hours in single file, almost over the same ground, and then up came the swag-bags...empty. Didn't they say things, the naughty boys.

"Shut down that bloody mike, Sparks, the P.M.G. may be wiggin'."

Even my ears tingled.

Aye, they're queer things, the little tail-waggers, almost as hard to catch as they are to understand.

Where do they go? Heaven knows sometimes, we can't find them. These periods are called 'slack fishing', and it is because of this mysterious 'fish movement' that trawlers are now fitted with radiotelephony.

During slack fishing that telephone loud-speaker blares incessantly; moans, curses, cat-calls; everybody screaming for information, and long ears wiggin' for the slightest hint.

Each of us carries a codebook and a list of pals' names. That code is known only to the chosen few, and we exchange good tidings when the fish are about.

We also carry a black list...in our heads, and fishermen have long memories. We help those who help us, irrespective of creed or country.

There are others. Aye, there are others! Telephone fishermen we call them...'lug wiggers'...'glass skiters'. We have other names for the bastards. Ask the P.M.G! These swine batten on the brains and experience of others.

When their cod-ends come up empty their lousy mugs are never away from the mouthpiece of the 'phone, screaming for information. But when they strike swag they shut down the speaker and lock the mike up until they've cleaned up the patch. They go further than that, some of them; they send out a bluff, a 'deaf 'un', false information, and fetch other ships steaming on to barren ground when they're ready to move off themselves. Several wasted hours steaming means that the other poor blighters will have a few hundred baskets less on their tally sheet when the gaffers compare the catch of the different ships at the end of the trip. And that means the sack for some.

These are some of the dirty tricks of this game in which only figures count.

The reason…Competition…And the fact that there are more skippers on shore than there are at sea.

'Catch fish or get out!' But that principle, in effect, applies to all classes of business, and I don't hold that we've any grouse against the gaffers. I like it, and it's the only system possible in this gamble. But still, the competition between skipper and skipper, ship and ship, reaches almost savage intensity at times. That's why we have 'Football Ships' and 'Cricket Ships'. That's why we fish on until we're nearly blown off the face of the bloody waters, in blizzard, fog, and hurricane. The fellow who runs for shelter as soon as old Feathery Legs snoops around soon finds himself sheltering under the lee of the dock offices looking for a ship. That anchorage can be just as barren and cold and as merciless as any in the Arctic wastes. By heavens, it can.

We can't all be crack skippers. Fishermen are born, not made, and I reckon that applies to all master craftsmen. There are men who possess fish sense, and this allied to 'fish fever', the urge to sweep hell if need be for fish, simply for the thrill of the hazard, are the two essentials which spell success or failure.

The successful skippers read the 'fish sign' in a thousand different ways. The gulls, the wind, currents, tides, the depth of water, the nature of the bottom, the type of fish caught in certain patches, the nature of the food in their bellies exposed by the guttin' knife, these factors and a thousand others supply information which can only come after years of battling and bitter experience. A crack fisherman must know the ocean bottom as well as our brass-buttoned brothers of the Merchant and Navy Services, bless 'em, are expected to know the top. Yow!

I have trawled along the lip of a marine mountain covered by 200 fathoms (1,200 feet) of water, on what was veritably a narrow mountain pass, scooping up hard sprags (cod) and ducks (haddocks), whilst another fellow, towing abeam and scraping my paint, has hauled in with barely enough fish in his cod-end to feed the ship's cat. His net-bobbins were rolling along further down the slopes of that hidden mountain. He didn't know the ledge was there. I did. That made all the difference.

When we find these little gold-mines we drop a dan buoy to mark the spot, and stay there until the fish move. Can you blame us if we keep the information under our crust, or at least share the knowledge only with those who are ever ready to share with us?

Fish are timid creatures, easily scared, and quick to flash their little tails in flight. That's why we keep a code book, so's the 'Telephone Armada' won't pick up the wirelessed information and come steaming down on the pitch.

Imagine the thunder on the ocean bed when the ponderous bobbins of a hundred gigantic nets come crashing along. Add to that noise the threshing of a hundred propellers churning the water up above. Then remember that each net is as long and wide as a street, sweeping up fish in hundreds of thousands, towing for miles over an area wide as a town, then try and reckon how long it'll take to wipe up, or scare away, a shoal of fish.

How'd you like someone to barge into your garden and pinch all your vegetables? How'd you like a steam-roller to come threshing through your flower beds?

Eh? Would you swear? Would you curse?

When it happens, as it often does, we curse the wireless, loud and long, and I know some skippers who never use it, trip in, trip out, 'cause of the long ears of the 'Telephone Armada'. Yow!

Aye, we curse the wireless sometimes, but yet it's the greatest thing that's ever happened to us. Away down North in these desolate, lonely, storm-swept seas, towing all along in the eternal darkness of the Arctic night, it becomes our sole and only link with civilization. We feel very far away from home, and from the wife and kiddies sometimes, but that black box seems to keep us in touch somehow, and helps us to carry on. Aye, it makes things easier some-times.

I remember Christmas morning, come two years ago, I was down there off Bear Island, nigh 75° North, and never a sight of land or living thing had we seen after leaving the Humber, only the gulls, and I'd been on the bridge for near sixty hours without a blink.

Down below, in the fish-pounds, for'ard, the lads were reeling like drunken men, the decks awash, swirling high as their armpits, and icy cold. At night we are lit up like a little town, and under the gleaming arc lights the water glistened and sparkled as it streamed down their oilskins in cascades.

They'd been on that lurchin', heaving deck, exposed to the full fury of a nor'-east gale nigh as long as I'd been on the bridge, guttin' and mendin', shootin' and hauling, cleaning and packing, and never a word of complaint.

Fish had been scarce, and there's no sleep or rest for trawlermen until we find them. No, no sleep nor rest till we find them.

I'd forgotten it was Christmas morning 'till Sparks tuned into National and I heard the church bells come pealing over the air.

That did it!

"All hands turn-in!" Then I cursed.

"Damn the sprags, and blast fishing…and blow, roll, howl" (to Old Feathery) "and be damned to you!"

I'd had enough, but I ordered all hands on to the bridge and handed round the grog. They all sat down in the wheelhouse, the water gathering around them in pools from their dripping oilskins, and there we sat for a spell listening to the distant thrum of an old, old hymn. Both trawls were stowed, the engines silent, we were laid-to, riding it out head to wind, a lone ship in a stark dead world, and before the last notes of that hymn died away every man-jack in that little wheelhouse was fast asleep.

Fast asleep!

That's how we spend Christmas sometimes.

But now I must leave you for a spell, it's time to haul the trawl.

"Stand by all hands!…Haulo!"

Chapter 2

A GRUESOME FIND

Aboard S.T. Arsenal.
Trawling Lat. 62° 25" N. Long 41° 15" W.

A change in the weather since my last entry in this log…Fog! Old Feathery Legs playing his trump card. The Bad Weather Devil knows we don't mind where the hell we go as long as we see the way.

See! I can only just see the outline of the foremast from the bridge, and there's a hundred other ships all round me, blaring away ten to the dozen, all with their trawls out, and crackin'.

We don't stop, not even for fog. If we hit anything…! Hope the other fellow gets our stem and we don't get his in our belly. I'd rather hit him in the guts, amidships, rather haul his brats aboard us, than become his guests.

Most of my crew have been 'Orphans of the Storm' more than once. They prefer their own kips, wet or dry, so its two long blasts every two minutes, and ears and eyes straining…straining.

Two long blasts! Ears! Eyes! Two long blasts Ears! Eyes! Just as long as the fog lasts…and never let up, 'cause the other blighter may be saving whistle steam.

We've towed thirty miles to the nor'ard since my last yarn with you, but still we can't catch up with the tail-waggers. Slack fishing! Darned slack fishing, that's what we call this lousy game today.

But here's a message for me over the radiotelephone, on trawler wavelength 140 M. Listen in and learn how a trawlerman helps a pal.

"Hello! Hello! Hello! *Arsenal*! *Arsenal*! *Arsenal*…Huddersfield… *Arsenal*… Huddersfield…*Arsenal*…Hello! Hello!…Are you receiving me, please?…Over to you, *Arsenal*! Over!"

"Hello! Hello! Hello! Huddersfield! Huddersfield!…*Arsenal*! *Arsenal*!…Yes, I'm getting you O.K. posh…O.K. posh…Back to you,

Huddersfield!…Over !"

Silence for a moment. Then I recognize the voice of my pal, Skipper Charlie Higgins. The message comes over in a slow drawl. I can hear him yawn. His voice trails…Weariness ! His fish-holds are full, the trip nearing its end. He's been towing for ten days, and I'll wager my last kroner he hasn't had twenty-four hours sleep during the whole of the time. Yow!

"Good morning, Albert! Charlie this end. Just heard you've fog where you are, and no fishka about. Clear as a bell over here, Albert. Sun shining. We've opened a fish shop. Fifty baskets last haul, forty of sprags (cod), ten of ducks (haddocks). I've dropped the old blister. (Dan Buoy). Come along and see what the sun looks like, Albert. Switch over to Sparks, and I'll give you a snap! I've finished…Over!"

My wireless operator gets crackin' before the last sentence dies on the air. A few quick twists of-a dial on the wireless direction finder, and he has 'snapped' the other fellow's position. Marvellous! Yes, almost uncanny! Don't ask me how it's done. Ask Marconi!

"Huddersfield Town fifteen miles to the so'-east'ard, Skipper, half a point starboard!"

O.K. Sparks.

"Stand by, all hands!" The brats appear on the deck as if by magic, headed by Abe, my mate.

Stretching taut along the decks, from stem to stern, the great trawl warps are straining ominously, like giant fiddle-strings. The brats eye these devil strings warily. They cannot understand the order yet. The net may be fast on some rock or wreckage far below, and if those warps snap…! They can cut a man clean in two as easy as knife cuts butter. That happens sometimes. You will see it happen later on.

They say there's no discipline on a trawler! Watch these lads leap…

"Haulo!"

Like famished gulls on fish offal, each to his station, before the order leaves my mouth. "Heave, you blighters!"

We're steaming, lads…goin' sun-bathing for a spell. But I don't call them blighters, although the word begins with a 'B'.

The whirring roar and rattle of winch and bollards drown my voice. The hiss of the twanging warps rises high above the screaming of circling gulls, and swishing waters, as they take the strain of the ponderous gear towing astern.

Crash! A mighty thud shakes the ship from stem to keelson as the massive iron-shod doors for'ard smashes home in the gallows. Crash! The second door smashes home, and again the ship shudders.

Then slowly the giant net appears above the surface of the boiling surf. The headline and upper floats first. Then the wings, the belly, the cod-end, and finally the massive steel bobbins…Old Neptune's beads.

"Steady! Easy on the brakes!…Easy, damn you!"

A moment of tense silence. This is men's work. Men's work ! Two of my crew are not yet seventeen, one is only fifteen. My fifteen-year-old must sometimes struggle with a cod bigger than himself. Every lad has long since reached manhood.

These ponderous steel bobbins, each weighing 100 pounds and numbering twenty, must be heaved aboard first, before the net can be retrieved from the water.

A huge gilson hook appears from the heavens, attached to steel warps from the swaying masthead.

Quickly this is attached to the warp which threads the bobbins.

"Heave!"

The winch whirrs again. The giant beads swing over the rails, poised on the edge.

Swinging death!

These bobbins must be lowered into the scuppers of the ship, between the engine casing and the rails, a space less than three feet wide. The crew line this narrow alley-way, cumbered by clumsy oilskins and thigh-high sea-boots, backs hard pressed against the casing, arms and hands outstretched, white, tense faces and staring eyes glued on those great steel balls. It is their job to prevent these bobbins from crashing against the casing, and thus damaging the ship. They must act like lightning on the instant they swing clear of the rail. The man at the winch must lower slowly, gradually, one eye on the lurching rail. He must time the release of the winch brake as the ship rolls away, and downwards from the men.

If he misjudges that time by a hair-breadth, aye, less than a split second, if the ship suddenly lurches as the bobbins drop, these great steel balls will flatten the men to pulp against the iron casing of the engine room.

"Lower!" A yell of derision, savage in relief. "Heave!"

The metallic crashing of steel against steel! Our decks are of steel, as the hearts of our lads must be.

Aye, finely tempered steel, and never found wanting.

All this takes place within seconds, and never a breath between.

Men's work! Aye, men's work! Imagine it in storm, blizzard, and fog. These devil beads claim many a brave young life.

The price of fish!

"Some people go to sea for pleasure, but we go to hell for nowt."

Swan song of the Northern Trawl.

I seem to remember that I haven't introduced myself yet. Well, I'm forty-seven years of age, married, four children, three girls and a boy, 5 ft. 7 in. in height, 49 inches round the chest, and proportionately streamlined. The wife says: "Once round my chest, twice round the Grimsby Docks".

I wish that was all I had to tell you about Albert Hutchinson. That's not false modesty, either. There are better men than me waiting to play their part in this log. We've all got nicknames, and I know the brats call me 'Hurricane'. You'll find out why presently.

Well, let's get crackin'

I started this lousy fishing game when I was fifteen, thirty-one years ago, and spent the first week afloat lying on the fo'c'sle floor with my head in a bucket. Yow!

That's practically all I remember about my first trip on a trawler, that and the smell of tarry bilge, rope yarn, paint, stinking fish, burning tallow, sea-drenched clothes, and the fact that we got shoaled in the Humber homeward bound, nearly turned turtle, had to be towed off by a tug, and a kettle of boiling water fell off the fo'c'sle stove and scalded my left arm and wrist. Otherwise the voyage was uneventful. Yow!

These things didn't worry me much. No! My sole and only interest was that damned bucket…the inside of it. No mother ever hugged a first-born as I hugged that cold zinc pail.

There was almost as much water in that fo'c'sle as there was in the sea outside, and dimly focussed on my memory (but almost dwarfed by the bucket) I remember that dark, dank, evil-smelling, lousy hole, with odds and ends of boots and cans washing eternally across the floor, banging against my prostrate body…and the bucket. With each pitch and roll of that heaving, lurching ship I slid, on my bum, from one side to the other. I never once stood upright during that time. Not once. I couldn't. It took me all my time to crawl.

After a week I recovered a little, but I was so infernally weak that my legs hadn't the strength to support my body on the heaving decks. It also required the arm biceps of a gorilla to claw on to the life-lines. So, after one crack, I crawled back to my bucket, and hugged it to the end of the voyage.

There was never much in it, as I couldn't hit it, and my belly was empty. Still, it gave me confidence.

That's all for the first voyage.

I often wish I'd taken that bucket home and kept it. It would be on my sideboard now. On a silver stand… And if ever my lad had expressed the least desire to follow in the old man's footsteps I'd have crowned him with it. Aye, I'd have crowned him with it. Yow!

Mention of the 'Old Man' reminds me of the best pal I ever had…my own dad. He kept a little retail fish shop in Grimsby, and although he was only a humble chap I must spare a word for him. At any rate, he'd more sense than me. He sold fish, but let others catch it.

He gave me everything that a lad could wish for, and never once lifted his hand to me.

Best of all memories of him, misty memories now, 'cause I lost him when I was only ten, was his hearty laugh. He was always laughing. That laugh, and a barrow-load of apples(?), are as fresh in my mind as they were when I was six years of age. As I close my eyes now I can see that hawker's barrow, with 'Strawberry Bob' pushing behind, come trundling down our street. Dad and I were standing in the door of the shop enjoying the sunshine of a warm spring morning. Mother was busy inside serving a customer.

The sun fair glinted on those apples. I'd never seen any so big and red. They were nearly as red as Bob's nose. We called him 'Strawberry' 'cause he'd a big, mauve-coloured wart on his snout. Yow! That wart used to fascinate me.

"Gae's penny for apple, Dad?" I said, my mouth fair waterin' as Bob drew nearer.

Out broke the laugh. "Apples!" Dad gurgled, looking down his nose at me. "Apples!" he boomed again.

His hand dived for his pocket. "Hey, Bob!" he spluttered, his sides shaking. "Gae our lad apple, will yuh! …Gae'm big een, Bob, the biggest thou's got on't barrow, an' see it's ripe, Bob, aye, see it's ripe."

Then Dad roared again.

I remember Bob looked at my father queer-like, and a wink must have passed, but I didn't see it. I was alongside the barrow like a shot, holding out the penny.

As a youngster I was inclined to quick temper, and as soon as Bob placed the fruit in my eager paw several things happened very quickly. I took one great bite, the juice squirted up my vents, and the next second 'Strawberry Bob' was picking the remainder of his over-ripe tomato out of his left eye. As I tore up the street with the hawker astern…he was about ten knots slower and never caught up…I heard Dad's loud laughter, like the blare of a liner's siren, far in the wake, and I've never liked tomatoes since that day I mistook them for the fruit that got old Adam adrift.

My mother is still alive, Grannie now to all of us since the coming of my three lassies, and the lad.

The old eyes still grow a little moist when we speak of Dad, as we sometimes do. She knits all my jerseys and sea-socks. That's her job. I always find time to go and see her at the end of every trip. When the winter storms lash the Humber, and that dire message comes thrumming over the wireless, "Gale warning !" I've always the feeling that Grannie, as she bends over her knittin', sends up a simple prayer for all our lads down North. I know she does, and I don't know which job is the hardest when Old Feathery's doin' his stuff...we fellows down there fightin' him, or our wimmen-folk sittin' quietly knittin' at home.

I don't think I'd like to change places. Would you?

That bucket scared me a bit, but I went back for some more, and I made my second trip to sea as a deckie-apprentice on the steam trawler *Kalmere*, a vessel about half the size of my present ship.

The *Kalmere* was commanded by Skipper Sam Amos, a famous old Humber trawlerman still well remembered. The Old Man treated me with every kindness. I owe a lot to Sam. He had me on the bridge whenever I could be spared from the deck, teaching me navigation and the mysteries of the lead-line. I will explain the lead-line later, when I take command again.

In my early days a deckie-apprentice was paid 3s. 6d. a trip, no matter how long the voyage lasted, and when I drew my first settlings I thought I had the Bank of England in my pocket.

Lads of the same age today, now called deckie learners, are paid 15s. weekly, and with 'liver' money their weekly wages average about 22s., but we'll have more to say about this wage question later.

I must have been born for the game, for very early on my blood was afire with the lure and hazard of the gamble...Fish-fever.

Watching the green swirl of the swag-bag shooting above the heaving waters give me a kick which has never waned with the passing years.

"Stand by all hands!...Haulo !" Pulses leap, and men spring like pouncing tigers when that order rings out. Death stalks at the heel of the laggard on the iron, sea-swept decks of a lurching trawler.

All hands are on deck to haul, and the trawler is stopped before the steam winches are put into action to wind up the great steel warps dragging the net. An eerie silence descends on the vessel for a second, with not a sign of life or movement on the sea or in the air. Then a strange thing happens. I believe the gaffer, Sir John Marsden, has mentioned it in the foreword of this book, but it will bear repeating.

I've seen it so often, and it still remains mysterious to me, particularly when we're trawling alone. At the first sound of the winch, no matter how far we may be from land, a white army of gulls swoop over the horizon.

The winch is their dinner bell.

Down they come...flocking, circling, wheeling, 'keening', their fluttering wings and shrill, weird cries rising high above the rattle, whirr, and twang of winch and warp.

Music of the Northern Trawl!

The extreme end of the bag, the cod-end, rises about thirty feet from the ship's side, and long before it appears above the surface of the sea this patch of water is always white with eager, excited birds. They always know the precise, exact spot where it will rise.

Then sometimes another strange thing may happen, a sight which always makes the Skipper sing. If it is a big bag, as the net nears the surface and the pressure of water lessens, particularly if the fish have been brought from a very deep bottom, say 200 fathoms (1,200 feet), air rushes into the bladders of the fish, causing distension, and the bag shoots to the surface with the speed of an express train, scattering the birds like flying spindrift. I've seen a bag shoot high above the surface of the water, nearly on a level with the bridge, with over a ton of fish inside, smashing back into the sea, sending up a wave high as the masthead.

A normal bag rises slowly; birds can see this fathoms deep, and as they spot the white sheen of the glistening fish, their excited squealing is almost deafening. Every eye on board is riveted on that net, and no gambler ever watched a card up-turned with greater eagerness than a trawlerman as that swag-bag surges above the waves.

The next problem is to get it aboard. The loot still belongs to Old Father Nep until the swag is safely in the fish-pounds.

Each brat to his allotted task, and one deckie secures the cod-end by means of a gilson hook attached to a wire rope leading to a block near the top of the mast.

"Heave away!" Again the winches whirr. Up she comes, streaming cascades of water, filled with squirming, fighting tail-waggers.

Slowly, foot-by-foot, it is hauled up the ship's side, until it is clear of the rail. For one tense, breathless moment it swings, pendulum-like, over the fish-pounds.

This operation takes about three minutes. The Skipper's heart ceases to beat until that great bag is safely over the rolling rail.

Excitement! Tense! Breath-taking!

That bag often splits, with a clap loud as a thunder-burst, scattering the fish over the surface of the waters.

Three hours battling for nowt!

Swear! Curse! Rave! Blast!

Aye, for at least three solid hours…and never repeat the same word twice. Yow

Safely aboard, another deckie dives under the swaying bag and makes a grab at the rope securing the cod-end. This rope (and the tying of it is a work of art) contains no knot, but merely a succession of twists and turns. The bo'sun is responsible for this job, or the 'Third Hand', as we call him. Sometimes this knot comes adrift when towing. When that happens the fish escape, the bag comes up empty…and the Skipper eats the Bo'sun.

That's all part of the gamble, one of the blanks. There are seventy-five cards in a 'Trawlerman's Pack.'

Seventy-four are blanks.

Aye, our hearts sing when that tumbling mass of squirming fish lands with a squelchy thud on the iron casing of the foredeck. That makes the game worthwhile. It feels good to be alive when these pounds are full to the brim. I've seen the whole of the for'ard deck knee-deep with fish.

At night, under the glare of the electric light, those masses of white, writhing bellies, the sheen of squirming, lashing tails, glinting with a thousand points of phosphorus, gives me a thrill I've never found ashore.

Aye, when the fish are about, it gets you, this game.

Holds you! Keeps you! Heart, body, aye, and soul

There's no escape once the fish-fever's in a man's blood.

No escape! No escape! We're here until Old Feathery claims us.

We find other things besides fish in the swag-bag, gruesome things, sometimes. I had one eerie experience as a lad, which still makes the hair rise on the old crust when I think about it. Yow! By heavens, it still makes my blood run thin.

We had just hauled. The swag-bag was swinging safely inboard over the pounds, cascading the usual waterfall and filled with wriggling sprags.

It was night, but as clear as day, with a full moon and nary a cloud in the sky. We were far north, nigh 72°, and down there the full moon appears three times larger than it does back home, and twice as clear.

The loneliness down there, it clings. One can actually 'feel it.' The stillness also, that sings, when the ship's laid, and the engines are silent. The beat of a seagull's wings are like velvet these nights, especially if there's ice around. And a man's voice, that travels far across the seas in calm.

Desolation! That's the word, and the silence, my God!

Desolation.

I don't notice it so much now, but as a lad it sometimes made my spine grow cold.

Sometimes we laid all night in the ice-pack. Sometimes those that went in never came out.

Men have lost their reason these nights, too, screaming aloud to break that awful, unseen curtain of stillness.

Well, there was the bag, swaying gently over the fish-pounds, and the moon, clear and wan.

"Albert, open the cod-end! It's about time y'larned, lad."

The Skipper's voice made me leap. It echoed far over the pulsating sea.

I'd never opened the bag before, but I had the strength of a young bull, and soon had the ropes undone.

I leapt clear as the fish crashed out, but a big sprag, nigh large as myself, caught me in the small of the back, and hurled me into the scuppers. I sat for a moment dazed, my eyes closed, for my crust had smacked hard against the iron rail, and it hurt. I opened my eyes, slowly . . . and I saw it. My yell might have been heard at the Pole.

By blazes, I got off the mark ten times faster than I did when I had old Strawberry Bob steaming astern. Yow!

A woman fell out of that net, naked as the day she was born, and there she was sat, with her back against the ship's side, her nose almost touching mine...and her throat slit from ear to ear.

We dumped her back in the briny, and no questions asked. Had the Skipper kept her aboard, aye, even for an hour, he would have fished alone.

I know it is generally believed that fish will eat human bodies. We fishermen know different. Sharks, and fish in the waters up South, may do, and certain kinds of shellfish, perhaps, but down North the fish won't eat human flesh. As a matter of fact I'm inclined to believe that our own particular tail-waggers, the haddock, cod, halibut and catfish, the kind we catch most, won't eat dead meat of any kind, because we sometimes bring up whole cows and. sheep in the trawl, blown off the mountains along the Iceland coast; and generally find the flesh untouched.

Incidentally, the blue-cats, and tiger-cats are the fisherman's favourite dish, and no sweeter nor cleaner fish come out of the seas. The sea-cats, ugly, almost repulsive in appearance, live only on the choicest shell-fish... mussels, limpets, and oysters. Their deadly teeth can pulp a shell as easy as a man's teeth shears cheese. Later on in this yarn, when I become Skipper again, we will witness these sea-devils in action in our fish-pounds.

Our pal, the haddock, 'duck' for short, and 'jumbo' for the large variety, lives on seaweed, sand eels, and marine plants, and is the 'timid victim of every cannibal fish of the seas.

The guttin' knife lays bare these secrets.

Master Cod, our friend the Sprag, on the other hand, is a cannibal... and some. In the larger variety, cod sometimes eight feet in length and weighing 12 stone we often find as many as twenty smaller fish in his belly. He invariably falls out of the net with a 6-pound victim sticking in his gaping maw.

But let's get back to that first ship of mine.

On another voyage during my cub days, one of the crew died whilst we were fishing off Iceland. We packed the body in the ice-hold until the end of the trip. An air of gloom always descends on the ship on these occasions, and a trawlerman would rather sail with the devil aboard than with a dead mate.

Still, we never like leaving one behind. We called in at Stromness, Orkney Islands, and the Skipper had a coffin made with a small, square pane of glass in the lid near the head so that the relatives in Grimsby would be able to see the face without opening the coffin. I had a peep through the little coffin window at our dead pal, but only one. That was enough.

Homeward bound, we stowed the coffin under the whaleback, near the entrance to the crew's quarters for'ard. Passing that sinister black shape at night 'tween watches wanted a helofa lot of courage. Once I had made the plunge for the fo'c'sle stairs I usually fell, stem over stern, down the whole damned flight of steps, landing with a frenzied yell and crash at the bottom…much to the delight of my sleeping mates. At least I assumed they were asleep before I arrived.

I was darned glad when the light of Spurn Head showed up a-starboard that trip. Yow!

One night a human skull fell out of the swag-bag. About an hour later, when the last fish had been gutted, cleaned and stowed away, and we were all ready to go below for a rodger (sleep), one of the trimmers passed along the deck, making aft towards the engine-room.

"Fifty baskets, Skipper, ten of ducks, forty of sprags! All stowed!" sang out the Mate to the Skipper on the bridge.

"O.K., Mister Mate. All hands turn-in."

A second later the decks were in darkness, except for the faint reflection of the navigation and towing lights, perched high on the for'mast head.

The night was inky black. Not even a star showed overhead. The glittering pin-points of phosphorus from the scattered fish offal lying around made the decks appear as if studded with diamonds.

We rubbed the human skull on the outside with phosphorus to show up the bony outline. Next we stuck a small piece of lighted candle inside the lower jaws to light the empty nose and eye sockets.

Then we carefully placed the gleaming, grisly relic on the top-centre of the whaleback, hard over the entrance to the crew's quarters.

We knew that the trimmer had gone aft to relieve his mate in the stokehold. We also knew that the other trimmer would steam for'ard towards that lovely skull with all the knots he'd got as soon as relieved. They like their rodger, the black squad. The deckies never waste an opportunity of baiting the black squad, albeit generally good-naturedly. Here was an opportunity in a million. So, like silent ghosts, we all crept into the shadows and waited.

Along came the other trimmer, black as night himself. He stopped dead in his tracks as soon as he saw that gleaming death's-head staring down at him out of the darkness. For maybe a second he remained as still and motionless as a statue. Then.

Booo-o-ooo! Boo-o-o-ooo! We all moaned in chorus. Boo-oo!

Mister Black shot back along that deck quicker than light travels, yelling blue murder. Help! Murder! Police! He roused the ship, and the Skipper and Chief Engineer raised hell, especially when the trimmer flatly refused to sleep for'ard again.

The Old Man had to find him a kip in the cabin. There he remained in comfort 'til the end of the trip. He had the last laugh. His mate tried the same dodge, went squealing aft one night, and swore he'd seen a ghost perched on the whaleback. The Old Man clouted him with a 10-lb. catfish.

But in the old days, even less so than today, there was little time for by-play.

Work! Work! Work! Day and night, night and day.

The eternal grind! Ceaseless! Savage! Relentless! Back-aching, heart-breaking! Hands so cut and torn, the wounds kept everlastingly raw and open by the salt brine of the sea that, at the end of every trip, the pain was so ghastly we couldn't untie our mufflers even.

Sometimes we've had to feed a man because the festering wounds on his torn hands made it impossible for him to wield knife, fork, or spoon. It's still the same today.

Tired! I've seen a circle of men around the mess-table asleep before the cook had even got the soup on the table. I've looked across my soup bowl and laughed, when I've seen a deckies' nose nod nearer and nearer his soup basin, awaking with a jerk only when his snout came in contact with the hot liquid.

Aye, I've often laughed at that . . . and the next second my own head has drooped down and down, and a second later my own nose had come in contact with the scalding soup in front of me.

Why have I stuck it so long? Because, as I've said before, there's a fascination about this game, a powerful, hypnotical force that well-nigh enslaves a man, and the more the kicks the better you like it.

Aye, there's a spell down North of 65° that holds a man just as long as the red blood courses through his veins, and providing I can cheat Old Feathery, and that's saying a mouthful, I shall be content to remain 'til the end.

Chapter 3

THE BOGEY MAN

Aboard S.T. Arsenal.
Trawling Lat. 62° 20" N. Long 41° 25" W.

In the preceding chapter I told you about a bucket, and my cub experience as a trawlerman. There's only one road leads to the bridge on this job...from the deck, and the fish pounds. No one can give you a leg-up either. Even if your father's the gaffer of a hundred ships he can't show you the road to the tail-waggers. No, you must travel that road alone, and it's a long, hard, dirty passage with Old Feathery Legs either sitting astern, or leering for'ard on the whaleback ready to give you a clout if you ease a yard.

Long before 1914 I had been through the mill, gaining all my experience with the Northern Trawl, first as Apprentice, then Deckie, Third Hand (Bos'un), then Mate, and I've never fished nearer home than 62° North. The farthest north I've been is 82°, and if you look at a chart you'll find that the Pole is not very far beyond.

I was mate when War broke out, but I at once dropped my rank and joined up as a Matlow, as the lowest rating in the Navy is called.

'Johnny-the-One', at Chatham, the Admiral in charge, soon discovered that I held a Mate's ticket, and within three months I was decked out in braid and brass.

That rig felt damned uncomfortable in more ways than one, but as several of my pals were poshed up at the same time, we weathered the chaff of hundreds of other trawlermen who were still in the more comfortable bell-bottoms of the matlow.

Shortly before my promotion I met another great pal...my wife, and a few hours before I sailed for that mysterious sea 'Destination Unknown' we were married in Chatham.

Allow me to switch off the course a little.

We parted at once, and I'm afraid her life has just been one long parting from her man.

A few weeks ago, for the purpose of this log, she reckoned up the number of years we'd been together in twenty-five years of married life.

Counting that tragic tally in days, tragic for her, aye, and adding even the precious hours, it works out at a little less than four and a half years.

Aye, my lass knows the price of fish all right, and the next time you sit down to that tasty morsel of cod or haddock, spare a thought for that army of lonely wimmen who sit at home and wait. They wait a long, long time, some of those brave lassies, listening for their man's footsteps, but all they ever hear again, far too many of them, is the eerie moan of the wind and the sough of the lonely Northern Seas.

Sob stuff! Aye, maybe it is, but then we hear plenty of sobs up Humber way. Aye, plenty!

Now don't misunderstand me when I write this: the War meant nothing to us fishermen, apart from the loss of brave ships and men, of course. It was simply just another job of work, a darned sight easier, and less dangerous, aye, less dangerous, than our everyday calling.

We are always at war, and in regions and seas which spew death and maiming in far more countless and fearsome ways than all the lethal weapons ever devised by the devilry of man.

True, we swept the deadly, hidden mine from the ocean highways; our little ships cluttered round the merchantmen, easy fodder for torpedoes, and welcome, as long as the big sister reached safe anchorage with food for the wimmen and kids, and stores for Tommy and Jack.

But we didn't expect medals for that. No, we didn't expect medals for that.

The berg and the ice-pack takes up far more sea-room than a submarine or battleship. They stay put in black-squall and fog, and they don't take prisoners. No, they don't take prisoners, and I'd rather chance meeting torpedoes or mine in the wide, open sea, than hitting a 'blinder', a hidden rock, in a black blizzard or winter gale somewhere North of 75°. As for shells, well some of us dodge a few of these in peace time when flat fish are scarce, and bogey-man snoops around when we're digging them out inside the limit line.

Hardships of war! Why, lord love a sprag, I grew fat, my muscles soft, and I nearly slept my brains away, except for the last few months of that show.

I'll tell you about that presently.

We generally laid-to all night, when sweeping for mines, with our crusts on the feathers, and we'd no warps to watch, no nets to mend, and mines don't want guttin'. Easy! Dead easy! Why, when we're fishing we get about one hour's rodger in twenty-four, if we're lucky, and often in winter we're on the bridge for three, four, aye, and sometimes five days and nights without a blink of sleep.

We lost men and ships, but we're always losing men and ships. Three winters ago, in 1935, we lost eight ships and sixty-three men from the Humber alone, and when I come to publish our losses since the War I think you'll agree that the price of fish is the price of men's lives. Aye, and the price of women's hearts as well, and broken homes, and fatherless kiddies.

About Christmas time last year the *Sheffield Wednesday*, my ship then, limped through the lock-pits at Grimsby Docks, nearly every rivet in her stem adrift. For a thousand miles we were battered by a 100-mile-an-hour hurricane, great mountains of waves, high as the masthead, sweeping the ship continuously from stem to stern. It was impossible to see a yard for the swirling spray, and how the bridge held God alone knows.

The bridge windows were boarded, of course, and for three days and nights I had my eyes glued to a peep-hole the size of a shilling, and down below, on the foredeck, it was like looking into a great tub of boiling soap suds. The wind never eased a bloody inch 'til the welcome light of Spurn Head showed up on our starboard quarter, and it was only by the grace of God we ever reached there at all.

In thirty-one years' battling in these accursed seas we had weathered the most terrible storm of my experience, and that's worth a page on its own. Entering the Pentland Firth-'Hell's Gates', we call that lousy death-trap-we picked up a message from the *Amethyst*. She'd got through the Firth and was somewhere ahead.

"Require immediate assistance. Boiler shifted. Listing badly. Hurry! Hurry!"

Hurry! We were all out but barely making two knots, and we knew that we'd heard the last of the *Amethyst*.

So it proved. There was only the silence after that...The silence

When we limped into the lock-pits a crowd of silent, white-faced wimmen were waiting on the quayside. They knew that we must have been near the stricken ship when the last message came through.

Any news? Any news?

No, no news!

I'll never forget that woman's cry, and I repeat it here! "Them that want fish let them catch it, I say!" she screamed. Then her sobs, deep and heart breaking: "Where's my man? Where's my man? Oh, God, where's my man!"

But no one could answer that terrible cry.

Aye, peace and war, it makes little difference to our wimmen folk... little difference.

The war record of my comrades has been told in cold official language, and may be read in any public library. "Gentlemen unafraid," some poet chap called us, but the Brass Hats sometimes called us other names.

They didn't like us much because we didn't care for brass, and persisted in calling each other Bob and Charlie irrespective of pomp and rank. Apart from that they paid us the compliment of saying that: "Y-Section played their part nobly, in sweeping the sea highway clear of enemy mines, escorting merchantmen, and in the thousand and one duties for which their small craft were best suited."

When that notice was plastered up on the wall, down by the Grimsby Docks, some of our lads cheered (a few made rude blurts), and I remember someone yelling out, glimpsing the signature of a famous Admiral at the bottom of the bill

"Johnny-Number-One, you old basket, you've said a mouthful."

Aye, reckon 'Johnny-the-One' has said it all, which saves me a job. But have you noticed two of the words on that bill?...Small craft?

Small craft, huh! Jumping blazes!

By hell, get this! For nine months I sailed the Mediterranean, looking for submarines, mind you - keep that well in mind - in a 70-foot wooden drifter, forty years old, speed 7 knots, bunker capacity 10 tons, and armed with only one obsolete 3-pounder gun.

Every blasted plank in that bloody old barge was warped with age. Her bottom was literally peppered with worm-holes. If we'd fired that gun (we tried but didn't succeed, thank God), the blinking ship would have fallen to pieces, and if we'd met a surface U-boat its backwash would have sunk us. Yow!

Roll! Leak! Her pump was broken, and most of our time was occupied, very fully occupied, baling her out with hand-buckets.

I never slept a wink on that - that - for heaven's sake, allow me to describe her in fisherman's language.

She was called the *Bendox* . . . officially. What we didn't call her wouldn't take up half-an-inch of space in this book. The only dry spot on that infernal water-tub was the masthead.

I was Mate, and when Armistice was declared the Skipper received orders to join a convoy of ten trawlers, then in Malta, proceeding to Falmouth for demobilization. The convoy was under the command of a Lieutenant, R.N., also in a trawler, and 'Jimmy-the-One' boarded the *Bendox* an hour before we were due to sail from the Island for home.

"What's your speed, Skipper?" demanded Jimmy blandly, speaking as if he had a walnut in his affected mug.

"Seven knots!" growled the Old Man. Then he spat. "When the fires are alight," he added, and spat again...to windward. The Royal Navy

44

skipped to lee, ducking to dodge the spray.

"Are you trying to be funny, Skipper?" Jimmy began, then backed full astern as the Skipper spat again. "Or are you merely being rude?" he added, from a distance.

"Rude!" The Old Man foamed.

That got the Old Man's door down properly. Curse! I thought I knew the language backwards, but I discovered I hadn't even started to learn it.

"Rude!" howled the Skipper, sticking his chin under the Navy's nose. "Rude!" he snarled, waving one great fist in the air. "The boiler on this bloody ship's under the water-line, mister," raved the Old Man, advancing until his nose was only about an inch from the nose of the Lieutenant's.

Jimmy-the-One stood fast, feet firmly planted apart, but as the Old Man's chin advanced with each spluttered curse, Jimmy's body, from the waist-line, curved steadily backwards, in an effort to get as far away from the spray as his dignity would allow; until he had the greatest difficulty in keeping his balance.

"Below the bloody water-line, mister!" the Skipper snarled again, "and not on the bloody masthead, mister," he hissed, his voice steadily soaring, "and there's a thousand bloody rat holes in her blasted bottom, mister"- their noses were now touching - "and every bloody plank on this jumped-up, blasted barge is busted, mister, busted, mister" - the Old Man again spat - "and the water comes in, mister, and coal and bloody water won't mix, mister." The Naval back steadily wilted, further and further back, until it almost formed a half-circle. "And when we get fed-up baling her out, mister" - the Skipper brought both fists into play - "we turn in, mister and blast the bloody ship, mister, and blast the bloody Navy, mister – and Lloyd George!"

The Royal Navy suddenly unbalanced, and staggered rapidly backwards, only the rails saving him from falling flat on his back. The next second, with becoming dignity, he steamed across the gangplank.

"And blast you, mister!" the Old Man screamed, as 'Jimmy' beat it back up the quay.

At Gib., homeward bound, and it took us a month to get there, the Lieutenant did his darnedest to get rid of us and go on with the faster ships, but Johnny-the-One, the Admiral in charge of the station, wouldn't agree, and we were still wallowing astern of the convoy when we entered the Bay of Biscay.

It was February, and without warning, a nor'-easterly buster hit us head on, and for fifty-six hours we worked like fiends, baling for our lives in the teeth of the gale without a moment let-up. The crew numbered ten hands, and as she sank lower and lower in the water every moment we expected that blasted tub to sink beneath us and leave us sitting on top of the blinking briny. Yow!

When the gale abated we were alone, the rest of the convoy scattered, and the most amazing part of this experience was that the leaky old *Bendox* was the first of the convoy to reach Falmouth.

We arrived on Good Friday morning, 1919, after a passage lasting nine weeks (think of it), and all that day, one at a time, the remainder of the convoy limped in, well battered by the storm, and all amazed to see us lying safe and snug in harbour.

Now listen to this, and then bless all the Brass Hats, you old sweats, who may read: Within twelve hours of landing in England, after an absence of two years, remember that, I had an experience over which I still ponder sometimes when I'm alone on the bridge down North. It still awes me, and I'm afraid the minds of some men are too deep, too profound, for we simple fisherfolk to fathom.

The majority of the men of the convoy belonged to Grimsby, and a few hours after we landed we were each granted Fourteen days' leave, and as we were issued with single railway tickets we thought the War had finished for us. Not so. Those other minds I mentioned just now were busy at work. A few hours after we landed home we all received urgent telegrams recalling us to Falmouth.

Excitement! The news flashed round Grimsby like wild-fire. "War with the Russians!" That was it!

Half the town saw us off. The station was crowded with weeping wimmen and wailing kids. There were rebels amongst the wimmen as well "Don't go! It's a damned shame! Don't go 'til your leave's up!"

A Brass Hat met us at Falmouth.

"Where's the war!" we yelled in chorus, heads out of the carriage windows, as the train slowed down.

"War!"

"Aye, war, lad! Why have you brought us back?"

We all fell in a dead faint when we got the answer to that one.

"Medical inspection! The regulations state very clearly that no man returning from Foreign Service must be granted leave or discharge without being medically examined."

"But we've been home! What the hell's the rule about that?"

"Fall in!"

After our strip-tease we made for the first pub we could find in Falmouth, and we were so mazed we got tight, started an argument amongst ourselves, which had something to do with the regulations, only my mind's not too clear on that point, but I have a faint recollection that several of our lads had to go back for another medical examination, and stitches, before we again steamed home for Grimsby that night. I know we looked for that damned Brass Hat, when we were tight, but we couldn't find him.

Back home again, the wife and I planned a nice holiday prior to the job of fishing.

But that wonderful mind was still working. Three days after our second arrival home we each again received urgent telegrams recalling us to Falmouth.

We all complied. That must go to our credit considering the treatment we'd received, but going down in the train we decided to start a real war on our own in Falmouth if any bloody Brass Hat even breathed the word 'inspection.'

The second recall might easily have been postponed until our well-earned leave had expired, and a little foresight in the first place might have saved the State several hundreds of pounds in wasted telegrams and railway fares.

Johnny-the-One met us again, and we were ordered to take our ships to their various home ports.

The *Bendox* belonged to Frazerburgh. When we nosed her home the dock was crammed with all kinds, shapes and sizes of craft, all showing scars of battle. We shoved her in amongst the bunch, made her fast, grabbed our sea-bags, left the home fires burning, gave her a fisherman's farewell, and how then steamed for the railway station…and Grimsby.

No, we didn't even pull the ruddy fires out. They're still burning, and welcome, for all I know, or - care.

Several weeks later I was again in jersey, oilskins, and sea-boots, and eager to get crackin' with the old swag-bag. I made several uneventful voyages, and then came a little affair which nearly landed me in the salt-mines of Siberia. I've never tossed a coin since. I prefer to decide my own destiny, now, and not leave it to chance, luck, fate, or what other name we care to give it.

Skipper Charlie Watson, or Big Charlie, as he is known from the Humber to the Pole, a Swede, was in command of the Steam Trawler *Redoubtable*, and when he asked me to go as Mate I jumped at the opportunity of sailing with a man who is recognized as one of the best fishermen sailing the Northern Seas. I also knew that the big Swede was absolutely fearless, and that he'd go to hell and back rather than come home with empty fish-pounds. That suited my mood. I'd a young family at home, and sweeping up mines had proved less profitable than digging up sprags.

It was December when we clawed down the Humber, thick of fog, and although under way we hadn't decided where we were going. That's one kick we get out of this game denied our brass-buttoned brothers. Every trip we make is a fresh adventure. Once a trawler leaves the lock-pits her

Skipper may guide her stem wherever he has a mind, and the gaffer will ask no questions providing she steams back with her holds full of ducks and sprags. The Skipper and Mate share the profits, just as they bear the losses, but we'll deal with this dry subject later. This is a red-raw adventure.

"Curse this damned soup, Albert," said Charlie, his nose glued to the bridge window, one great paw clutching the whistle cord. I gave the wheel a turn as a grey shape loomed up out of the murk.

"Where are we going, Skipper?" I asked a minute later. The full-throated blare of the whistle drowned my voice, and another minute passed before he asked:

"Where shall we go, Albert...the White Sea?"

The White Sea? Hell! It was December, the White Sea lies North of 70°, would probably be icebound in places, and Englishmen and British ships were decidedly unpopular in that jealously guarded Russian pond. No trawler had been there since the War, and I knew that our Insurance didn't cover the risks still there in plenty on account of the Russian Revolution. Yet the Big Swede asked the question as quietly and calmly as if he'd suggested, "Let's go over to Cleethorpe Sands, Albert."

Again the whistle blared, and Charlie half-turned towards the wheel. "Shall we go dere, Albert, eh?"

"Makes no difference to me, Charlie," said I. "Where you go, I go!"

He grabbed my hand. "Dat's the spirit, son!"

The fog lifted a little as we neared the river mouth, and dimly, aport, the yellow flash of the Spurn Lightship filtered through the eddying banks of mist. A second later the Swede rang the engine-telegraph from slow to half ahead, then I saw him glance at the swaying compass overhead.

When we swept into the North Sea the weather was fine and clear, the moon full, off the starboard quarter.

"What course, Skipper?" I asked.

Again the Swede glanced upwards, the subdued light of the compass showing a face square and strong as his massive frame.

"I tell you what, Albert," he said, his hand diving for his pocket. "We toss for it, yes?"

O.K., Skipper!

"Heads, Iceland!...Tails, White Sea!"

It came down tails, so we slewed her stem in a line with the North Cape of Norway, and the bridge telegraph clanged to full ahead.

A few days later we sharpened the big chopper aft. I believe I've described the big doors, or otter-boards, which keep the mouth of the great net open in the water. I've also described the 3½-in. steel warps, or ropes, which drag the ponderous gear astern. When these doors are being dragged through the water, the tremendous resistance set up reduces the speed of the vessel, even when the engines are full out, to three and a half miles an hour, which is scarcely more than a crawl. Hence, every trawler carries an enormous chopper aft, ready to chop the towing warps in twain if ever we get in a jam and want to go full ahead, or astern, on the instant. It takes from ten to twenty minutes to haul in the trawl with the steam-winch, and that chopper has saved many a trawler from destruction. Better to lose the gear than ship and men's lives.

Several Skippers have found that chopper useful for another purpose. Flat fish-soles, plaice, and turbot-always bring a good price on the market. But they're exasperating little beggars. They like to lie smug and cosy in shallow water within the limit-line, three miles from the shore. I think they must know we are not allowed to take the big swag-bag in there. But sometimes we drift in by accident, especially if it's foggy and very dark, and when the bogeyman suddenly flashes his spotlight, and starts barking, that chopper comes in useful. It's better to chop the gear and run away, and live to poach another day. If bogey-man catches us, why he takes our gear away, and all our fish, and a thousand pounds in hard cash as well.

That's why some skippers stop…and fight, and some time ago a skipper pal of mine was sentenced to six years imprisonment because he arranged a naval battle off his own bat down North. But that can come later.

Shortly after the War flat fish were selling in England at from £6 to £10 per box, and on that voyage to the White Sea I knew that Big Charlie was dreaming of lemons.

The weather was foul when we reached the White Sea, freezing hard, and fishing was slack to begin.

One night, black as the pit, we decided to lay near the Russian coast-line. Beyond the curtain of bur own navigation lights there was nothing but inky darkness; not even a star showing.

Charlie and I were on the bridge when suddenly the glare of a searchlight stabbed the darkness, blinding us for a moment, and a few seconds later a shell came screaming over our bows.

Running away would have meant certain destruction. That shot was fired at almost point-blank range. We accepted the warning and sat tight.

The wind had eased, and presently the lean, grey hulk of a gun-boat loomed up on our starboard quarter, and very quickly afterwards a Russian Naval Officer jumped over our rails, followed by an escort of armed matlows. The officer could speak English.

"You are in the territorial waters of the Union of Soviet Russia, Captain!" he snapped tersely. "What is your business here?"

"I ran in for shelter!" replied Charlie, just as tersely.

"Shelter!" the Officer laughed scornfully. "It is not because you want to see things, Skipper, what d'you call it in English…to spy, eh?"

"Spy, be damned!" growled Charlie. "I'm a fisherman, as you can see." Charlie waved his arms.

"Search the ship; you will find only fish."

"Fish! Ah, yes, Skipper!" The Russian glanced up at the wireless aerial. "That is also for fish, eh?"

Charlie could also speak Russian, and for several minutes both men held a heated argument on the bridge, whilst I stood by, busy with my thoughts, and trying to sense how the situation was drifting. I certainly had visions of bad weather ahead. Life was cheap in Russia these days. It was also highly probable that they had never seen a trawler with wireless. Not many had wireless in those days. That gear would naturally make them suspect that it was there for only one purpose, and as British trawlers had long since given the White Sea a wide berth, and as the Russians and the Soviet then hated everything English, anyway, it was only natural that they would suspect our guise was camouflage.

In that God-forsaken hole anything might happen to us, and our ship would come in useful to them once they got rid of the crew. Very useful. A rich prize worth having.

The salt-mines or a firing squad! Which?

And so the two men argued, but when Charlie commenced cursing in English I knew we were booked for a Russian harbour…or worse.

I was right. Half an hour after that shell came whining over our stem we were steaming astern of the gun-boat, under arrest, an armed escort aboard.

Towards morning a gale sprung up and it commenced to blow like the Wrath of God. But the big Swede blew harder. Charlie cursed the escort in English, Swedish and Russian, occasionally blasting the Captain of the gun-boat through the megaphone. He cursed them all through the Kola inlet, and he didn't let-up until we steamed in to Murmansk Harbour.

Immediately we arrived the ship was lashed to the quay with about a hundred ropes and hawsers. Our decks looked as if a great spider had wrapped a monstrous web around them. The ground was six inches deep in snow, and an enormous big sentry, complete with rifle and bayonet, was posted on the quay alongside the ship. His black whiskers completely hid his face, and his long overcoat, trailing on the heels of his thigh boots, made him appear half as tall as the mast.

A Russian Military Officer marched aboard, complete with armed escort, paraded the crew, and warned us that the sentry had orders to shoot anyone who attempted to leave the ship.

The day following our arrival Charlie was hauled before a Military Tribunal for examination. The President, a Russian woman in uniform, told him quite bluntly that she suspected we were spies.

"I will forward your statement to Moscow, Captain," said the lady, at the end of several hours' grilling. Then she grimly added: "I will also inform the Soviet that your vessel carries an extremely up-to-date wireless installation." Yow!

Six days passed, the big Swede appearing before the Tribunal daily. On Christmas Day the cold was so intense that the steam from the dinner-pots froze on the galley walls, and the crew, hardened as we were, muffled up before appearing on deck.

Aye, we thought we were tough guys, until we saw that big, black-bearded Russian giant lie full stretch on the snow at night on the quay, and curl up like a huge black bear. When he did that on Christmas night, with the temperature thirty below, we expected to see him frozen stiff in the morning.

He was on duty for six solid days and nights without being relieved, feeding off our grub, sleeping in the snow every night, with only his overcoat and his black beard for covering. But he was on the spot every morning, shaking the snow out of his whiskers, and looking for English grub.

Murmansk was a town of the dead at night. It would have been lonely without that sentry. The Arctic night was long, as well, and for nearly sixteen hours out of every twenty-four he was the only living thing we saw, except ourselves.

Aye, it would be lonely without him, but still we got a nice keen edge on the chopper.

He was very fond of rum and coffee. When we learnt his limit, we gave the chopper another grind.

It took nearly half a jar of rum one night, and when morning came we missed him.

Aye, we missed the lad, but we didn't miss him as much as he must have missed us. The ends of the ropes were still hanging to the ship as we steamed down the Kola Inlet, the vessel in darkness, taking a risk of bumping into another ship rather than the salt-mines of Siberia. Hell for leather we ran for the friendly coast of Norway, and England.

Off the North Cape we risked recapture, shot the trawl, and in three hauls the swag-bag came up with 700 boxes of tail-waggers, which made £750.

Not bad for a few hours' work, especially with a Soviet gun-boat chasing up astern.

Chapter 4

MYSTERY OF THE DEEP

Aboard S.T. Arsenal.
Trawling Lat. 62° 15" N. Long 42° 20" W.

Sentiment! Sentiment in this fishin' game means the dole. I've written that before, but I'm writing it again to refresh your minds. Our ships are of iron, from stem to keelson, even the masts and bridge, as the hearts of the men that sail them must be. I've written that before, as well.

Aye, iron-hard, and forged with fire.

This Iceland coast, where I'm fishing now, stretches for 2,000 unbroken miles. We call it 'The Graveyard'. In winter, for nine solid months, that treacherous surf-line, littered with 'blinders', is hidden either by thick, impenetrable fog, or blizzard, or the eternal darkness of the Arctic night, and wind-swept, during most of this period, by the devastating fury of North Atlantic gales, or the full force of tidal swell.

Old Feathery's Hell's Legions

In winter it never lets up. No, it never lets up, and pitted here and there along this coast, if you look close enough, you'll see the gaunt, skeleton remains of what were once little trawlers, fitting tombstones indeed for those of my pals who have gone a-fishing.

Men say these waters are haunted. They speak of a ghost ship that comes gliding abeam out of fog and blizzard, the starboard trawl towing astern, and nary a soul aboard.

Personally, I've never seen it. But maybe it's lucky for us we haven't time to think of ghosts when our trawls are sweeping these cursed waters, and even if they have brought us gold we can never feel grateful, for we have paid for every single cent in blood.

Aye, in blood! In broken and battered ships. In broken hearts and homes. In fine young lives, the flower of our manhood, cut off afore they'd even started to live.

The price of fish! The toll of lives and brave ships which these treacherous seas have claimed will never be told.

Names come back to me. Aye, names come back to me, names that are more than memories. My old pipe draws hard, and makes a queer, sucking noise in the stem when I think o' some of the brave lads that Old Feathery has claimed in recent years.

Let these figures speak

In ten years, from the Humber area alone, Hull and Grimsby, we have lost 517 men killed and seriously disabled, and 37 ships totally wrecked.

The number of ships and men saved from shipwreck by the fearless and unselfish efforts of my comrades' tallies far above that figure. That tally also will never be told.

The winter of 1935 was the blackest since the War. Here's the toll:

The *Langanes*, *Jeria*, *Juliana*, *Merivale*, *Edgar Wallace*, *Lochard*, *Picador*, *Amethyst*, *Sabric*, and *Admiral Collingwood*.

That was the price the wimmen up Humber way paid for fish in 1935.

The crew of each ship averaged eighteen hands, the majority married men with families. All were lost with the exception of two on the *Edgar Wallace* and six on the *Picador*.

Brave lads, gallant ships! They steamed down the Humber one morning on a job of work, turned left, sailed on, on down North, and that was the last that the eyes of mortal man saw of them.

Not a sign! Not a spar! Only the silence of those desolate, accursed seas. Only the silence.

Aye, lucky for us, perhaps, that our job requires savage concentration. Lucky for us that we must wage ceaseless and relentless warfare against that Black Devil down North. Lucky for us we haven't much time to muse over the fate of our comrades, otherwise our blood might turn to water, and those that wanted fish would have to come and get them themselves.

Aye, iron ships and iron men. There's room for none others in this gamble. I'd learnt that long before I stepped on this bridge.

Iron! Why, during the first year I was in command no deckie would sail with me twice. At the end of every trip my crew left in a body, and every time I steamed down the Humber I'd a fresh crew aboard.

I drove the deckies until they were too tired to sleep. I drove them 'til they fell down in the fish-pounds. I fished on, fair or foul, just as long as the ship's keel kept in the water. They left me, but they didn't hate me. They understood!

On shore in Grimsby we're a happy crowd. Jack's as good as his master, and all ranks mix together from the gaffers down to the humblest deckie. But at sea discipline on a trawler becomes ruthless, relentless. All individual friendship ceases.

The reason…Competition

I have already said, without exaggeration, that the spirit of competition which exists between individual skippers is almost savage in its intensity, and now that I've got back on this course I shall have to be very careful. This subject arouses more argument, more bitter, heated bickering amongst fishermen than all other aspects of our job put together, and every word I write will be examined with a microscope.

Let's examine it in detail. I think it will surprise as well as interest. At least it may cause you to stop and think the next time you see the well-filled slabs in our retail fish-shops.

The latest trawlers each cost about £25,000 to build, a tidy sum to invest in the biggest gamble known to commerce. My own company, the Consolidated Fisheries, Ltd., the largest in the world, with Sir John Marsden as Chairman, own 120 vessels, chiefly sailing out of Grimsby, Swansea, and Lowestoft.

On all nett profits made by each ship the Skipper receives £10 in every £100 (10 per cent), and the Mate £7 (7 per cent).

These officers receive no salary. The remainder of the crew, the deck hands, are paid a salary of £2 weekly, and in addition twopence in every £ nett profit, and a share of liver money, which averages approximately about £3 each trip, sometimes more, but very seldom less. Their average wage works out at about £4 10s per week, and they earn every cent of it.

My present vessel, the *Arsenal*, eats up £150 per week in expenses, and this is about the average.

Thus, if the ship is absent from port for twenty-one days, the average time of an Icelandic fishing trip, the expenses generally total about £450, which means that if the fish caught is sold for less than that figure the Skipper and Mate not only do not receive any profit for their labour, but they actually finish owing a sum to the owners.

This is what we call 'settling under the red line.' It is also called several other names. The man who 'keeps on' settling under the red line soon changes his sea-boots for clogs, or worse.

Aye, when the gaffers tell a man 'Get yer clogs on,' there's a bitter taste in the mouth that wants some swallowing.

'Get yer clogs on' means a shore job on the pontoon, lumping… packing fish. Sometimes that job comes early on, when a man's still in his forties. Then we say he's been unlucky.

I've said that at sea there can be no sentiment in this game. The same applies ashore. If a skipper keeps coming back trip after trip with his fish-holds half empty, I don't think we can blame the gaffers if they ask him to change his sea-boots for clogs for a spell. This is a business, when all's said and done, and the gaffers are businessmen, or they, too, would be lumpin' on the pontoon.

Unlucky! Well, maybe yes, maybe no. Luck certainly plays a part in every gamble. It's possible for a man to come back with his hold crammed to the brim with swag, and then settle under that fatal line.

The market may be against him. It's possible for him to stand by and see half his catch sold at a penny per lb., or less, and the other half sent to the manure dump. We'll have something more to say about this later.

At sea, Old Feathery Legs, the Bad Weather Devil, has a big say in that thin red line. But then he treats us all alike, only he's a bit harder on the timid.

Again, I've already pointed out that it's possible for two trawlers to fish in line for hours on end, towing along practically the same course, and with the same length of warp out, yet the cod-end of one will come up filled with swag, and the other...empty!

Unlucky! But is it luck? The man behind the wheel on the lucky (?) vessel may know every stone, mound, and depression of his ground, lengthening or shortening his trawl warps according to necessity, whilst the other, not so well versed, may be towing blind, praying to heaven his net won't come fast on some jagged rock or other obstruction beneath the keel of his prancing ship.

There's also another kind of Skipper who finds his bunk a lot more comfortable than the bridge and lets the Mate dig out the sprags. There's not many of that kind, but there are a few, and the gaffers soon get to know them. The deckies yap when they get ashore.

An extra hour a day in that bunk means that the other fellow has maybe hauled up twenty baskets more, and at the end of a trip that score can total up to hundreds. A fatal difference.

The gaffers are only concerned with figures. Personally, I've never yet settled in debt. That remark will cause another uproar over the 'air.

"All trawlers calling the *Arsenal*! Lucky *Arsenal*! Lucky Hutch! Three loud blasts!"

I'll cause another uproar by claiming that the 'Share System' is the only system possible in this game.

The constant, competitive battle, fostered and encouraged by the gaffers, which means tireless effort, ceaseless toil, and days and nights without sleep or rest, is also a necessary part of this hazardous gamble. It may seem that I am flying the gaffer's pennant astern, when I make that statement, trawling for favour. But my pals will know different, and not even my lesser friends will be able to say that my record won't stand the strain. It's the uncertainty, the gamble, the hazard which makes us stick, and battle on. That's the sole incentive.

I've been lucky. Let's leave it at that. But even we lucky ones bitterly resent a damnable system which allows a man to settle below the red line, and receive not a cent for his labour.

That looks like a contradiction, and that's just our trouble. In our hearts we hate the system, loathe it, abhor it, and yet feel there is no other way. No there's no other way.

If any of my readers can suggest a remedy to this, our greatest problem, after reading the last word in this yarn, let him come right along to Grimsby. We'll all meet him at the station, gaffers included, with the town band, and our beer's the best in England. Come right along

No; if we care to be perfectly honest, we know that the gaffers are wise. In effect, they give us a ship worth a fortune, and once we steam through the dock lock-pits we can do what we like with it, go where we have a mind, and work when it suits us. They've had a few lessons.

More than one skipper has gone *touring*.

Then there's the human angle, and the gaffers are wise to that. I ought not to write the following, but, then, I'm thinking of my pals: A man must be of iron, absolutely fearless, and devoid of all sentiment when at sea to make good at this game.

More than that, he must give his whole heart, his body, aye, and his soul to the job. And if there's a harder, or a more dangerous on God's earth, lead me away from it.

No, to make good in this job, and to keep on this bridge, where I am now, a man must think only of fish, and if his heart's in the game', well, I reckon he's never happy unless that trawls on the bottom, the only place where it will catch fish.

It requires the stamina of an elephant to keep awake on this bridge sometimes, and it's a lonely job standing here for days and nights on end without once getting the old crust on the feathers, and not a soul to talk to, especially in the winter time when, trip in, trip out, we never see the light of day, maybe just a grey twilight for an hour towards noon which makes our world more lonely and ghost-like still.

The skipper's the only man in the wheelhouse when the trawl's astern. All the other hands are either on deck, guttin' or mendin', or turned-in; and when fish are scarce the Skipper stays put on the bridge until he finds them, or should do, even if he doesn't get blink or rest throughout the whole of the trip.

That's his job

There are thousands of men ashore kicking their heels in idleness, as good as the best afloat, simply because there aren't enough ships to go round. That naturally increases the competition. Many of these men are still young, in their forties, the victims of a new school of thought. Some of the gaffers nowadays, men who have never been to sea in their lives, and never intend to, the sons of better men who knew this game inside out, and learnt that lesson down North, where we are, prefer younger skippers, lads not yet in their thirties. That's also causing bitter argument in which the wimmen-folk take a lusty part, as they do in all our troubles, but this one, I believe, more so than in any other.

This particular type of gaffer, mostly young men themselves, say that the younger man can stick it better, and that it's only natural for the older men to ease down, and run for shelter when Old Feathery's doing his stuff.

In my opinion, no man should be on this bridge unless he's had at least fifteen years' experience on the deck, and has learned every trick of the game not only of fishing but of the weather. The younger man, desperately anxious to make good, sometimes take heedless and criminally foolish risks and is apt to forget there are other human beings besides himself on that ship. Many a young skipper has staked a chance on one more haul, ignoring, or scorning, if you like, the advice and warnings of more experienced men who knew he hadn't a hope in hell of getting away with it.

This game is all risks, winter or summer. We all take them, but it is only by hard and bitter experience that we learn the limit line. I've gone beyond it myself once or twice, forgetting that although it takes three months to build a trawler it takes less than a minute to sink her.

Old Feathery has a thousand different cards in his pack, and he plays them in a thousand different ways down North. But give the Old Devil his due, he always slings out a warning before he plays the ace. The man who ignores that warning is not 'daring' or 'fearless', tags we all like to have against our name in this game, but merely a fool, and the damnable part about his folly is that other men and ships have got to take even greater risks to get him out of a jam.

But let's go deeper into the science of fishing, from every angle, particularly for the benefit of the ambitious deckie who aspires to reach the bridge.

Fishing in the deep-sea waters is regarded by many in the same way as angling in the fresh-water stream-as the casting of nets or lines in the hope that the net or line may be pulled in again weighted with fish. Devout wishing is not unlawful, but devout wishing hooks no fish. The angler who baits his line with devout wishes some time or other is rewarded for his patience with a good catch. But he can all the less understand afterwards how comes it about that there are occasions when he draws an absolute blank. Is it that the fish are not there? Is it that they are not hungry? Is it that the meal offered is not sufficiently tempting? Or has the weather some malign and mystifying effect? To we fishermen who have pulled out

SKIPPER ALBERT HUTCHINSON
("Hurricane Hutch")

A little later, over the horizon came the smoke stacks

Down below in the fish pounds, for'ard, the lads
were reeling like drunken men, the decks awash.

He stopped dead in his tracks as soon as he saw that gleaming
death's head staring down at him out of the darkness.

Is this a cod – or isn't it

Ship covered in ice

Photograph of an iceberg taken during the author's last trip in northern waters.
"The iceberg takes up far more sea-room than a submarine or battleship"

Charlie and I were on the bridge when suddenly the glare of a search-light stabbed the darkness, blinding us for a moment.

their boats from the coves, and bays, knowing that ere morning they must catch fish for sale or the family would probably go without a meal, these questions have all needed answering. The sea fisherman who follows his pursuit as the means of getting a living cannot placidly regard blank days as a species of bad luck.

No! The catching of fish is a scientific problem, an exacting science, and until some of our lads get that into their thick nuts - well, they'll continue to wear clogs for seaboots.

In my younger days some of our methods were crude, but they helped us to catch fish.

When towing the trawl over the sea bottom, it was common practice in those days to place one's hand on the warp on the rail; vibrations were felt as the trawl heads passed over the various ridges, and in this manner a rough idea was formed as to the nature of the sea-bottom.

I have often placed my teeth on the trawl warp, with fingers in ears, and felt the vibration which was transmitted along it, and by this would ascertain the movements of the trawl heads on the sea bottom.

In the early exploring days on the new grounds in the North Sea these were some of the crude methods adopted in order to obtain our information.

The fishermen of Brixham and of Barking trawled their nets fathoms below, out of sight. Why was it that sometimes the net, when hauled, was full and at other times empty? Did the sea bottom vary? The fishermen 'listened in' by the only means in their power. In that way they discovered that there were rough grounds and smooth grounds. As time went on the ground was charted.

It was not until about the middle of the century that the rapid growth of the trawl fishery commenced.

The charts of the North Sea, which were published in 1847, gave very imperfect description as to the depth, banks, and deep gullies which were afterwards located, and the rough grounds where it was impossible to work the trawl nets. Several headlands and shoals had few warning lights or buoys to mark their locality by night or by day.

The currents of the ocean were imperfectly known, as also were the varying temperatures of the sea at different times of the year; and the salinity of the waters favourable for each kind of living creature was not known.

The fishermen had to be their own scientists. Navigation was a matter of thumb-rule with them. They made sounding leads, and with these not only discovered the varying depths of the water, but a little hollow in the lead brought up specimens of the sea bottom.

The discovery of the 'silver pits' brought wealth to some within the industry. It also taught that temperature of the water and salinity might explain how it was that fish migrated from place to place, and that food might be another great explanation of these migrations.

The unthinking man may regard deep-sea fishing as going out from port; casting overboard the trawl, towing it, and hauling again. Fish are not caught that way.

No! They are not caught that way.

The Skipper must decide what type of fish he desires to catch, must have some idea where to proceed for it, and must have some glimmer of knowledge how to discover it. Will it be found on the bank where he trawled a week or two before? It takes long years of experience to answer that question.

As I have written before, fish are sensitive to change of temperature, the flat fish particularly so, and we must depend to a great extent upon native wit for studying these matters. But such intricate problems as the migration of plaice, the distribution of plankton and other food, are quite beyond the average fisherman.

He has first of all to make a living, and it is to such men as the late Mr. Alward, of Grimsby, and Professor Buckland, both well-known names in the fishing industry - names that will never be forgotten by us - that credit is due to interesting scientists in this matter, and thus helping my comrades the better to wrest a living from the jealous seas. That is, those who have taken the trouble to learn the lesson taught by these great men.

It was Frank Buckland who said: "The natural conditions of the bottom of this great North Sea are, in a scientific sense, less known than the deserts of Sahara. Yet this great fish farm of Her Majesty's subjects is practically more important than the recent revelations made at a vast expense to the country of the abysmal depths of far-distant oceans."

Frank Buckland did a great deal to bring the study of the fisheries before the Government and others in this country. He was indebted greatly to the fishermen themselves for information regarding the bed of the North Sea and the habits of the fish there, but he brought a scientific mind to bear on the mass of information he received, and he co-ordinated and tabled the details in a way that was not possible on the part of the fishermen themselves.

The fisheries are not merely as old as the hills, they are older, for the first duty of primitive man was to secure food, and before he learnt the art of producing it by cultivation he would take the food that offered-the game of the forest, the fruits of the trees, and the fish from the waters.

We have disputes in these days, regarding the use of the trawl in various waters, disputes as to the size of the mesh in nets, and disputes as to other catching contrivances, and it was in 1376 that the fishermen in certain harbours and havens objected to what was apparently a trawl net, but which was called by the name of 'Wondyrechoun.' If the net was as unwieldy as its name, it must have been a fearsome weapon. The complaint was that it "destroyed the flowers of the land below water there, and also the spat of oysters, mussels and other fish, upon which the great fish are accustomed to be fed and nourished." This net brought up such an amount of small fish, it was alleged, that "they knew not what to do with them and that they feed and fat their pigs with them." In that way they foreshadowed the present day when fish meal is a very valuable food for pigs.

But enough of this subject. I had an object in stressing it at length. Perhaps you'll appreciate that object when you learn how I came to be known as 'Hurricane Hutch.'

As long as I live I will never forget the thrill of taking my own ship to sea. It was Christmas Eve as well, 1922, and I parted with the wife and kids at home. Our wimmen-folk never see us off; we generally leave as if we were just off across the street.

"Good luck, Albert! Good fishing, man…and…and…a safe return!" There was a catch in the lass's voice, but her eyes were shining just as bright as mine. She'd got the fish-fever bad as I had.

Well, step aboard, and into my wheelhouse.

There's very little ceremony when a trawlerman sets out to sea. As soon as we get aboard it's muffler, jersey, and sea-boots, and we seldom wash or shave, or undress, until we see the light of Spurn Head again, homeward bound. We can't spare the water to wash, but the salt water keeps us clean.

When we turn in, we kick off the sea-boots and untie the old muffler, and sleep, when we can, with one eye open, and both ears cocked, in case Old Feathery comes sneaking around without giving a bollo. Men must leap when that Black Devil's doing his stuff.

No bells are struck. No useless waste of words. No compliments. We save our breath to curse the weather and broken nets.

Navigation! I've heard it said we're fishermen first, and seamen afterwards. Well, maybe yes, maybe no! Our navigation might be counted crude by our brass-braided brothers of the Merchant Service and Navy, bless 'em, but we get there just the same even if we do go overland sometimes, as the crow flies.

I've chipped a few pieces off the Iceland coast, but I've never been greedy. We look at a chart about once a year, and when we do I reckon a piece of string or a match comes in handy for measurements.

Some of the old skippers, when they wanted a glint at a chart, as they very seldom carried them, used to stop a merchant ship and borrow a squint. Personally, I've seen a sextant once. But I've never used one. They're not much good when you can't see the sun for about nine months of the year.

One ship I sailed in sported an old alarm clock, generally run down. That was the only chronometer we possessed. We forget about the time until the fish-holds are full, or we're running short of coal and grub.

Compasses! These are generally several points out. Every sailor man knows there is more magnetic disturbances down North than in any other waters.

Barometers! Generally set fair when it's blowing like hell! Yow!

We shape our course by what is called 'dead reckoning', and the compass, lead, and log are sufficient for our wants. We can reach our grounds blindfold, as we must do often in blizzard and fog. We know the direction, and the number of miles, and the log, trailing astern, acts, in effect, precisely the same as the speedometer of a motorcar.

The lead is a big lead weight with a cavity at one end filled with grease. This is secured to hundreds of yards of rope marked in fathoms (6 ft.), and according to the depth of water, and the sort of mud, sand or shells which adhere to the grease, when it is cast on the bottom, we were able to tell just exactly where we were in the old days.

"Swing the lead!" the Skipper would sing out, maybe after steaming North for six days without catching a blink of land or sun. A few minutes later, when it was heaved up, one quick glance at the grease-filled cavity, and then: "O.K., we're here. Get crackin'…Shooto !"

Was that seamanship? Aye, it was, even if I say it myself. Consider the conditions we had to face more often than not…Storm, fog, blizzard, ice, winter darkness, uncharted rocks, faulty steering, compasses out of order, magnetic interference, currents, and tides might easily have landed us in hell, or off the north coast of America, instead of Iceland, had we been lacking in seamanship. I claim that boost for my pals. Still, we do admire our natty brothers of the Merchant Service, particularly their buttons, even if they do say we are fishermen first and seamen afterwards.

Today the echometer, an electric gadget which I can use but can't explain, takes the place of the lead.

My first command was the Steam Trawler *Venture*, and luck seemed dead against me as soon as I turned the stem of my ship into the Humber. We can only stay out for about thirty days at the most, on account of restricted coal and ice space, and every hour occupied on the outward and homeward passage means one hour less of fishing.

It took me ten precious days of terrific battling to reach my ground, the West Coast of Iceland, in the teeth of a nor'-westerly gale.

The Pentland Firth is shallow and narrow. Here the Atlantic tide sweeps through, and the ground swell lifts to tremendous heights, greatest of all seas on earth, and the most dangerous, even in summer sometimes. In a nor '-west winter gale the dread grandeur of these enormous sweeping breakers puts the fear of God into the heart of the most fearless man. But to reach my ground I either had to go round the Shetlands further north, and thus lose more precious hours, or fight my way through 'Hell's Gate'. I decided to take a chance, a dog's chance…I was a young skipper, desperately anxious to make good.

The gale whipped round to hurricane strength as I entered the treacherous channel, great seas crashing aboard, thudding against the bridge, the razor-edged snout of the *Venture* one minute pointing straight at the heavens, leaping, swooping, soaring, her stern submerged to the engine-room casing, the next, down, down, deep in the trough, completely hemmed by the mountainous waves. Again and again I was battered back, scarcely moving, and that treacherous death trap all but got me.

I got through, by the grace of God, but the weather was still foul when I reached my ground.

The majority of the ships in the vicinity were either laid, riding it out, or sheltering in near-by fiords.

I decided to fish…and damn the weather.

There was little daylight about this time. Only a grey twilight for an hour, and for five days I battled on with my decks awash to the level of the rails. The crew cursed and raved, and cursed again. I cursed louder, and drove them. I was out to justify my existence, to make my name.

To catch fish!

I had lost ten precious days. I might lose another ten going back, and I preferred sea-boots to clogs.

I generally tow for two and a half hours, and if the men jump to their jobs of shooting, hauling, and guttin', this generally allows an hour's sleep or rest between each haul, providing the nets don't come up split. When that happens no one leaves the deck on my ship until the damage is repaired, and sometimes that means an all-night job. In the meantime, the other trawl is on the bottom, the only place where it will catch fish, and the job of mending is interrupted between the usual hauls. A good crew of ten deckies will gut, clean, and stow a ton of fish in less than an hour, but that means graft, hard, savage graft under the best conditions.

In a winter gale north of 60°, without rest or sleep for days and nights on end, I defy any man to find a word in the English dictionary to describe the almost incredible hardships which our lads must endure to bring that tasty morsel of fish to your table.

What makes them stick? Don't they ever mutiny…rebel?

That's our secret…Trawlermen's Discipline.

The job must be done. Always that trawl must be on the bottom, and until we can control the elements…harness Old Feathery…we can't alter the conditions.

One Weak link, one man not pulling his weight when that ponderous gear's being shot or hauled, might mean death for all on board. The conditions we face eternally are savage, relentless, and must be faced in the same spirit…eternally.

If we get a laggard aboard, and he doesn't jump out of that bunk at the first word of command, and leap to his work, we drill the whole of the crew. Aye, we drill them, drive them, and one lesson in a lifetime is generally sufficient. Yow!

How? What's the method?

Instead of hauling every two and a half hours, a heart-breaking job at any time, I can haul that net every hour. Instead of putting the same net back in the water, I can order the opposite net to be shot, another heart-breaking task. I can also arrange a nice little split off my own bat by a wrong turn of the wheel. And if the brats catch up on me I can wait until they've got their crusts nicely on the pillow, and when I reckon they're asleep: "Stand by all hands. Stow both nets! We're steaming!"

That's how we maintain discipline. Never a word passed, except the order. The rest of the brats say all, and do all that is necessary to convince Mr. Laggard that there is only one law down North, and one way to fish.

Cruel! Hard! Relentless! Aye, maybe, but if anyone can teach me my job after thirty-one years on these waters I'll be pleased to meet him also up Humber way.

I lost my crew at the end of my first trip. They left in a body. They'd had enough. I lost many crews after that. But I brought back the goods, and the market was good to me. My first catch realized £1,450, of which, of course, I took £10 of every £100, and my name was second from the top on the settling sheet; high above that thin red line I was telling you about. Yow!

Only one man beat me, a crack skipper of many years' experience.

I was lucky. Let's leave it at that. But perhaps I ought not to leave it at that. We Skippers of the Consolidated have often to thank Big Bill Brackenbury, our outside manager and head fish-salesman, for getting that extra penny per pound out of the buyers which makes all the difference between settling either above or below the thin red line.

Over six feet in height, and powerfully built, 'Bull Brack', as he is known on the fish pontoon, sways the soulless buyers by the sheer force of his dominant personality.

His sales figures run into millions of pounds sterling yearly, and one of his record-breaking performances may read almost incredible. He actually sold 3,000 boxes of heading and filleting sprags in thirteen minutes on one occasion.

'Brack' works for his employers first (and last), but scrupulously fair and just, he has the respect of every buyer, small and large. They all know that they will get a square deal from 'Bull Brack,' and as I say, we Skippers of the Consolidated owe a lot to the man who controls the harvest of our endeavours.

Chapter 5

GENTLEMEN-UNAFRAID

Aboard S.T. Arsenal.
Trawling Lat. 62° 15" N. Long 42° 20" W.

When I made my last entry in this log we were fishing off the East Horns, Iceland. Since then we've towed a little to the Nor'ard, and I'm now in what we call the 'Bumping Ground', so called because the ocean bed in this little part of the Iceland pond is littered with rocks and wreckage.

Overnight the weather has changed from moderate to half-a-gale, and we're shipping it green.

Since 1 a.m. this morning-it is now 8 a.m. by the bridge clock-we've been dodging about, laying to, riding it out, and risking an occasional haul. That's not easy, when the ruddy sea's as high as the shore mountains, six miles off our starboard quarter, and the 'Highbury Lass' is chucking the water about.

The *Stoke City*, sister ship to the *Arsenal*, is towing just abeam of me, off the port quarter. I can barely see the tips of her masts as she wallows in the trough. She looks like a submarine with only the periscope showing. But watch her come up on the crest of the waves. Swoop! Leaping like a racing dolphin. Swish! Her razor-edged snout shears the green mountains in twain. Crash! Her foredeck awash to the rails. Toss! And she's dry as a bone.

Swoop! Swish! Crash! Go on, lass! Up, up and over. Up the City!

Run for shelter! She and her young skipper, Jack Evans, look you, 'ud sweep hell for sprags if need be, and the town of Stoke, and the football team, ought to be proud of their trawler namesake. She's done things, down here, nigh 70° North, unheard and unsung.

That reminds me…Incidentally, most of the football ships of the Consolidated Steam Fisheries have had visits from their namesake football teams, and several of the skippers have kicked off when their 'shore team' has been engaged at home against Grimsby Town F.C.

Naturally, we are always proud when our 'shore team' is on the winning side, even if they are playing Grimsby Town, and we follow the matches with the closest interest.

I was in command of the trawler *Sheffield Wednesday* last year when my shore team, then, was sent down into the second division, and over the 'air' the lads did a bit of leg-pulling. Listen-in "All trawlers calling *Sheffield Wednesday*! Hey! Hey! Albert...Hey! Hurricane! .Hey!... Second Division!...Get off this ruddy pitch! This is First Division!... Beat it...Over!

Believe me, even if I'm trawling at the North Pole next year when the *Arsenal*, my shore team now, win the cup and the league, I'll blow this darned whistle until there isn't an ounce of steam left in the boiler.

Yow!...Paddy, my chief engineer, won't mind.

Aye, the town of Stoke ought to be proud of their little trawler, and now I think it is time I introduced one or two of my pals into this yarn. I have only space to introduce one or two, but let their records speak for all.

Young Jack Evans was a proud lad when he sailed the latest football ship *Stoke City* down the Humber two years ago last January (1935) on her maiden voyage. Aye, he was that.

Two weeks later, shortly after dawn on 22nd January, he was battling for his life against a 100-mile-per-hour hurricane, fighting desperately to reach the shelter of Patriksfjord, a narrow inlet of water off the Coast of Iceland.

Overnight he had fished on until he was nearly blown off the face of the waters. But Jack is the type of skipper who has long since learnt the limit line, although he almost went beyond the limit that fatal morning.

He reached shelter, but only just, and when he let go his anchor, about 5 p.m. that afternoon, in the calm waters of the fjord, he found that several other trawlers had arrived in the safe haven before him.

It was mid-winter, pitch dark, and bitterly cold.

"We were dead beat, Albert," Jack told me later, "and I was looking forward to a nice long rodger, in the old bunk, clapping myself on the back because I'd managed to get in out of it, when a voice suddenly came over the loud-speaker behind me on the bridge."

That voice was from the Grimsby trawler *Jeria*. Somewhere out in these terrible seas a tremendous wave had crashed aboard, sweeping the funnel of the little vessel clean from its moorings, and leaving a gaping hole over the engine-room and boilers, down which the water was pouring with tremendous force.

The *Jeria* was commanded by Skipper Bill Emsley, and the

message ended:

"I am being driven ashore between Stalberg Light and Redsand Bay. Now about eight miles from the land. Require immediate assistance."

The lighthouse keeper at Patriksfjord also picked up the message, and at once warned all vessels that the gale was increasing outside, and that any attempt at rescue would be fraught with extreme danger.

Despite this warning, and without hesitation, Jack Evans hove anchor, and shortly afterwards the sturdy snout of the *Stoke City* was pointing seawards in answer to the call of her stricken sister. Two other vessels followed suit, both Yorkies from Hull, the *Lord Plender* and the *Beachflower*. Side by side, with only the faint glimmer of the dancing navigation lights showing, these three ships raced slap into the teeth of a North Atlantic hurricane, and every man aboard knew that the chances of rescuing the battered *Jeria* was a million to one against, with the same odds against their own vessels weathering those terrible seas.

An hour later, it was now about 6 p.m., all three vessels were still together, battling against a head wind which reduced their speed to less than five miles an hour.

Meanwhile, the *Jeria*, the great seas pouring into her gaping wound, was drifting nearer and nearer the terrible rocks of Stalberg Corner. Her batteries had given out, and by now she could only send messages and not receive.

"We can see the rocks. Hurry ! Hurry !"

No need to tell the *Stoke City* to hurry. Nearly every man aboard had relatives on the doomed *Jeria* and somewhere close at hand, on another vessel, two brothers of Skipper Bill Emsley were listening to that quiet voice they knew so well.

For another hour the Stoke battled on, every available hand down in the stokehold shovelling grimly for that last ounce of steam that might mean the difference between life and death for their helpless comrades.

Towards 8 p.m. the faint glimmer of the Stalberg lighthouse showed up through the blinding spindrift, three miles to the starboard off the Stoke's bow. Altering course, she slewed towards the land, and as she turned her head an enormous sea swept the vessel fore and aft, crashing against the bridge with tremendous force, heeling her over until her funnel was almost flat on the waters. For a moment she lay like a stricken thing, shuddering from stem to keelson.

"When that sea hit us, Albert, I was actually standing upright on the port wall of the bridge, the floor perpendicular and pointing straight at the heavens, clawing on to the wheel like grim death. God knows how she ever came up again."

But she came up, shaking her proud head, again slewing towards the land.

A minute later another wall of green, boiling surf caught her broadside on. Again she heeled at a sickening angle, the sea ripping the starboard trawl from its moorings, and causing damage which was later estimated at £400. Again she rose, snorting defiance, her storm-battered head pointing towards that faint glimmer of hope, and the spot where the *Jeria* must be.

Too late, Jack, too late

But yours was a gallant effort, equalled often, perhaps, in these cursed waters, but never surpassed.

No, never surpassed, lad.

Jack didn't hear the last message which came over the 'air.' He was too much occupied on the bridge.

But others did. Aye, others did.

"Good-bye to my wife . . . my kiddies! Goodbye, Grimsby! . . . Good-bye, Eng . . ." The last word was never completed.

After that . . . silence! Only the silence

All night long, buffeted unmercifully by the raging hurricane, the *Stoke City*, the *Lord Plender*, and the *Beachflower*, searched that deadly coastline, hugging the land as near as they dared, searching for a sign of the *Jeria*.

Towards dawn, the grey, ghost-like twilight of an Arctic day, the wind abated and the three ships clawed nearer still to the coastline.

Not a sign! Not a spar!

A few weeks later Alf Evans, Skipper of the *Jean Eva*, and brother of Jack, brought a great wreath from the people of Grimsby and dropped it on the waters near where we think the *Jeria* must lie.

We drop many wreaths on these desolate seas from up Humber way.

Before leaving his lodging to join the Grimsby trawler *Jeria*, as trimmer, the fate of Ronald F. Smith, a single man, was read in a tea-cup by his landlady. She saw in the tea-leaves a ship wrecked on the rocks. On the morning he sailed Smith had his breakfast, and just before leaving the house his landlady persuaded him to have a cup of tea. After he had drunk it he turned his cup down and said:

"Read this." His landlady looked at the tea-leaves in the cup and there she saw plainly a ship bumping against the rocks. When told what she had seen, Smith remarked, "Well, in case it's my ship, and I'm drowned, you had better have my sister's address so that you can send her my belongings." He thereupon wrote an address in Attleborough, Norfolk, on an envelope, and on the back of the envelope he wrote the word "*Jeria*".

Smith then left for sea and the incident passed from his landlady's mind until, on the night of Tuesday, 22nd January, at 11.30, when filling a kettle of water at the tap in the scullery of her house in Columbia Road, she declares she heard Smith's voice calling to her from the sinking ship.

Less than two weeks after the *Jeria* was wrecked, on 1st February, 1935, the Grimsby Trawler *Langanes* sent out an SOS that she had struck the rocks in a snow blizzard and was ashore off Dyrafjord, west coast of Iceland.

Over twenty trawlers raced to her rescue, and in the vanguard the dauntless *Stoke City*.

The vessel sent out an SOS about 7.30, and twenty minutes later sent out a further call, indicating that her hull was grinding badly on the rocks, and concluding with the appeal, "Come quickly." Then the wireless operator fixed his key so that the signals would give ships with direction finders the opportunity to locate the wreck. The signals were continued until 8 o'clock, when they ceased, owing, probably, to the transmitter having been put out of action by the sea.

At dawn on the 2nd February, Jack Evans reached the spot indicated in the wirelessed message. As he neared the coastline he at once saw that the ill-fated *Langanes* was hard on the rocks, and fast breaking up.

His glasses focussed the battered hulk, and he also quickly noticed that her boat had gone, and concluded that it had either been swept overboard, or the crew had taken to the smaller craft when the vessel first struck.

Then he peered closer and noticed a small, black speck clinging high in the rigging.

The wheelhouse and the funnel of the wrecked vessel had been carried away, and Jack decided that the crew had sought refuge in the rigging, and it was likely that they had been swept off by succeeding seas until now only one remained.

Meanwhile, another trawler, the *Bunsen*, of Hull, which had arrived before the *Stoke City*, had lowered a boat, manned by the Mate and two deckies. Tremendous seas were running, but these brave lads had faced them in an open boat, and were making desperate efforts, against almost incredible odds, to reach the last survivor of the *Langanes*. As the *Stoke City* crept nearer the wreck, the little boat, which was then being towed to windward by the *Bunsen*, suddenly turned turtle, casting the would-be rescuers into the ice-cold water. The Stoke was then dangerously close to a coast-line which is pitted with treacherous blinders (hidden rocks), but Skipper Evans rang his engines to full ahead, and swept towards the upturned boat. He succeeded in picking up two of the men by means of a life-line.

The Mate of the *Bunsen*, the third man, floated past the *Stoke* in sea-boots and oil-skin frock, but his ice-numbered fingers were unable to hold on to the life-line, and he was swept to his death.

The *Stoke* went on again and fired another lifeline to the lone figure clinging in the rigging of the *Langanes*.

No man will ever know his name.

All night long he had suffered the full fury of an Iceland blizzard, clinging desperately to that storm-battered wreckage, watching his comrades, one by one, torn from that lurching cordage, and he must have possessed the stamina of an elephant.

He was seen to claw on to the life-line, but his lifeless hands could not hold on. As it slid through his hands he made a last despairing effort to grab it with his teeth. The effort dislodged his foothold, and the next moment he fell into the churning seas, and was dashed to pieces on jagged rocks which litter this sinister coast.

Later, several bodies were picked up close in shore, horribly mutilated and beyond recognition. A small white cross on the cliff-top of that sullen coast marks the remains of the crew of the *Langanes*.

There are many white crosses along that barren coast.

Back at Grimsby the sad task of breaking the news to the bereaved relatives in our many disasters is always undertaken by that great Man of God, Mr. H. Pickering, the Port Missioner.

Women scream and faint when they see him coming down the street, and when he makes an ordinary call, he always shouts, long before he reaches the house, or maybe, from the bottom of the garden:

"It's all right-I've no bad news."

After the *Langanes* went down, Mr. Pickering was engaged all day on the Saturday, and far into the early hours of the Sunday morning, visiting the homes and condoling with the sufferers.

He carries a book-the death book-and here are a few extracts from the black pages of that terrible diary.

Our particular chapter is headed

THE WRECK OF THE *LANGANES*

The following is a list of the crew

Skipper Charles Patterson, 2, Fuller Street, Cleethorpes, married, family of seven, youngest aged 7.

Mate H. Sparrow, 122, Castle Street, Grimsby, married, and one child aged 8 months.

Chief Engineer C. Lax, 8, Constitutional Avenue, Cleethorpes, married, two children, aged 14 and 12.

Second Engineer R. Hyde, 186, Wellington Street, Grimsby, married, two children, aged 4 and 3.

C. Miller, 4, East Marsh Street, Grimsby, married.

W. Lawson, 10, Nacton Street, Grimsby, married.

C. Stephenson, Bettina, Yarborough Road, Grimsby, married.

J. Whitehouse, 37, Fuller Street, Cleethorpes, single.

J. Fleming, 223, Brereton Avenue, Cleethorpes, married, four children, aged 15, 13, 11, and 10 years.

N. Burrett, 228, Heneage Road, Grimsby, single.

A. Howard, 95, Nelson Street, married, four children, aged 9,4, 2, and II months.

H. Bale, 26, Albion Street.

W. Scathard, 15, Marshall Avenue, Grimsby, single.

Philip Patterson, the 19-year-old son of the skipper.

By this further disaster to Grimsby's trawling fleet nine wives are widowed, and there are nineteen children left fatherless.

The past twelve months has proved a black period for the port, for no fewer than eight trawlers have been lost along with fifty-three lives. Details are as follows

Date.		Lives lost.
Jan. 26th	Sabik	12
June 8th 1934	*Lord Birkenhead*	–
Oct. 9th, 1934	*Juliana*	14
Oct. 25th, 1934	*Holborn*	–
Oct. 29th, 1934	Macleay	–
Jan. 22nd, 1935	*Jeria*	13
Feb. 1st, 1935	*Lincolnshire*	–
Feb. 8th, 1935	*Langanes*	14

In addition, six men have lost their lives through being washed overboard, bringing the total for the twelve months to fifty-nine.

In the case of Mrs. Patterson, wife of the skipper of the *Langanes*, the circumstances are particularly distressing. The skipper had taken his son, Philip, as deckhand on the ill-fated voyage, and both are drowned.

An elder son, Charles, had sailed with his father in the ship, but on this occasion Charles remained ashore, and Philip went to sea. Mrs. Patterson has a family of seven, including a daughter who is married to the mate of a trawler.

After being out of employment for several months, H. Sparrow, the mate, made one trip in the *Franc Tireur* in the New Year, and then transferred to the *Langanes*, on which he was making his first voyage. He leaves a widow and a baby girl, aged eight months. When informed of the sad news by a neighbour, Mrs. Sparrow collapsed.

The former mate, named Marwood, had an accident on a previous trip, and was just too late to sign on for this trip. He went to sea in another ship.

Mrs. Stephenson, of "Bettina", Yarborough Road, has only been married five weeks. Her husband was making his first trip in the *Langanes* after serving in the *Blackburn Rovers*. Whilst in her he contracted influenza, and had to remain ashore for a week. On recovering, he signed on the *Langanes*.

The family of Clarence G. Lax (40), of Constitutional Avenue, Cleethorpes, has suffered the second bereavement within two days. Skipper Andrew Wilson Mair, of the drifter Swirl, who was lost in the Humber a week yesterday, was a brother-in-law. Another brother and brother-in-law were lost at sea together in 1920, when their trawler was blown up by a mine.

Mr. Lax was making his second trip in the *Langanes*.

Trimmer N. Burrett (29), was a single man and would have been married shortly.

Saturday was the sixth anniversary of Second Engineer R. Hyde's marriage, and Mrs. Hyde was looking forward to his return from this trip in order that the occasion might be properly celebrated. Two children are left fatherless.

James Whitehouse, a deckhand, was the son of the famous 'Jimmy' Whitehouse who formerly kept goal for Grimsby Town. Thirty-one years of age, James Whitehouse was single and had lived with his sister at 37 Fuller Street since her marriage ten years ago. Prior to the ill-fated voyage, Mr. Whitehouse had been sailing in the *Spurs*. He was at home a week before joining the *Langanes*, and he seemed uneasy about sailing in her; he had never experienced that feeling before, explained his sister.

John V. Fleming, another deckhand, who was a married man with four children, had previously been on the *Langanes* but he had had three trips on the Preston North End before his last voyage. His wife said he had a funny feeling about sailing in the *Langanes* again, but for the sake of his four children he joined her. Another member of the crew who said he was not going on the trip was A. Howard, a trimmer, and he voiced his feelings to a neighbour, who advised him to 'keep his sea legs.' The deceased replied jokingly: "Oh, they won't get me yet." He was a native of Lowestoft and this was his first trip on the *Langanes*. He had been shipwrecked four times off Iceland, and was a member of the crew when the first *Jeria* was wrecked.

Mrs. C. Miller, wife of the third hand, has had a double bereavement in a short time. Prior to hearing of her husband's death she lost her sister. Miller had been on the *Langanes* since July, and he told his wife that after that trip he would have a change. During the War, when serving on the *Belvoir Castle*, the vessel was torpedoed, and the skipper taken prisoner;

the crew were turned adrift.

The cook, H. Bale, was making his fourth trip on the ship. His wife lost her first husband at sea during the War.

.   .   .   .   .   .

Away back in 1889, the crew of the Grimsby trawler *Sando* were cut off from civilization for six months. She had been caught in a great ice-field far north, and although letters were handed to an Icelander to post the native had to walk a distance of three hundred miles, over an ice-bound country to carry out his task, and consequently, long before these messages reached Grimsby, the vessel had been given up as lost.

Meantime, the relatives of the stricken crew had gone into mourning, and when at last the men returned, several of the married members found that their wives had taken other spouses. How that state of affairs was readjusted had better be left to the imagination, but a very similar occurrence happened shortly after the War.

In 1923, the trawler *Sargon* left Grimsby in the early part of January for the White Sea fishing grounds with a crew of twelve hands, seven of whom are married men with families. She was reported at Lofoten, in Norway, on 2nd February, and should have been back again in Grimsby on or about 7th February. Between the two dates, however, the northern seas were swept by terrific gales, which caused considerable damage to shipping, and when the *Sargon* did not return to time hopes were held out that she had put into some foreign port for safety. As the days went by, and no further news was received concerning her whereabouts, there were gloomy forebodings, but it was not until a fortnight had elapsed that the owners and underwriters gave her up as lost and the families, with one or two exceptions, went into mourning.

But now let us board the *Sargon* on that eventful voyage.

Several days out from Grimsby she sighted the small Scotch trawler, the *Ethel Dutton*, flying distress signals. The latter had sprung a leak, and for nearly 100 miles the *Sargon* towed her disabled sister, in the teeth of a terrific gale, but, unfortunately, when within a few miles of the coast of Scotland, the *Ethel Dutton* sank and her crew, numbering nine hands, which had been taken aboard the *Sargon*, were landed at Leith.

The *Sargon* then steamed for her fishing ground, and she was next heard of at Lofoten, Norway.

Shortly after leaving Lofoten, on 2nd February, the vessel encountered a hurricane which blew her miles out of her course. The ship used all her coal in steaming against the big seas, and eventually she was carried into the North Atlantic out of the regular track of shipping.

The plight of the crew became more dangerous every hour, but by chopping up the small boat and all the woodwork, and burning her nets and hawsers, the skipper succeeded in keeping up a certain amount of steam and headed the vessel for Iceland. Food supplies gave out and for sixteen days the crew were compelled to exist on the fish from their catch.

Battling with the wind and battered by the heavy seas, the vessel ploughed her way through the storm, and it seemed as if there could only be one ending to the voyage, when suddenly the German trawler *Schlesvig -Holstein* hove into sight and towed her over 200 miles to safety.

She had been missing for over two months, and when the joyful news reached Grimsby from Reykjavik that the *Sargon* had just been towed into that port, there was some doubt as to whether a mistake had not been made, but another cable arrived shortly afterwards and placed the matter beyond doubt.

Immediately the owners were assured of the vessel's safety they lost no time in communicating the glad tidings to the members of the families concerned, and their grief was turned to joy. In the town and district the receipt of the news caused a tremendous sensation.

As in the case of the *Sando*, the majority of the relatives had gone into mourning. But there was one wife who never lost hope, and that was Mrs. Thomas, wife of the third hand-a bosun-of the *Sargon*.

She absolutely refused to believe that her husband had been drowned, and unlike other supposed 'widows,' she did not wear mourning, although, when asked to attend a memorial service which was to have been held at the Seamen's Mission, she confessed that she had looked in drapers' shop windows at mourning apparel.

Asked to account for her optimism Mrs. Thomas said that her husband had had so many escapes from death on the sea that she had a feeling he would walk in through the back door as usual.

"I knew the sea would never get him," continued Mrs. Thomas. "I often dreamed about him and I felt sure he would be drifting about somewhere. During the War William was mine-sweeping and he has been mentioned in despatches for saving life and rendering first aid."

Even whilst Thomas was in his teens he had a narrow escape from drowning, and about ten years ago, when a member of the crew of the steam trawler *Lacknia*, that vessel was run into by a steamer, the *Loch Lomond*, and she sank off Flamborough Head.

He had a similar experience with the *Freda*, and the crew in this case were taken into Yarmouth. Two years later the steam trawler *Derien* was sunk just off the Pier Head, and Mr. Thomas had to jump on to another boat to escape being drowned. Whilst minesweeping during the War a monitor was blown up near where his vessel lay, and he assisted in saving the lives of members of the crew.

After all these escapes is it any wonder that Mrs. Thomas never lost hope?

Mrs. McCarthy, the wife of the skipper of the *Sargon*, confessed that she had had some of her clothes dyed black, and that she had ordered a new black costume, but she could not believe the ship was lost.

A Mrs. Clifton, wife of the cook, was so completely satisfied that her husband had met his death that she sold up her home and was preparing to leave Grimsby to be with members of her family in London, when the announcement of the safety of the *Sargon* and crew reached her.

We get many of these little dramas down Humber way.

·　　·　　·　　·　　·　　·

There are thousands of fjords off the Norwegian coasts where we sometimes run for shelter to get out of the weather, but even these havens have proved death-traps on occasion, as witness the mysterious disaster which befell the trawler *Golden Deeps* three years ago.

The only survivors were Skipper Norman Rogers and two spare hands, Mr. Valentine Baker and Mr. Reginald Beales, and at the usual Board of Trade inquiry presided over by Superintendent Commander-Paymaster Malcolm Shankland, regarding the loss of the vessel and thirteen members of the crew, the following evidence was given, and I append it verbatim, as it may give the landsmen a slight conception of the terrible weather which sweeps these Northern coasts, and the dangers to be encountered when even riding safely (presumably) at anchor under the lee of the land.

Skipper Rogers stated that the *Golden Deeps* sailed from Grimsby on 24th October, 1935, for the White Sea. The voyage proceeded as usual, and about eight o'clock on 6th November the trawler left the fishing grounds at Fuglov Island to go to Breivik Fjord, on the West Norwegian coast in accordance with arrangements previously made to obtain information as to the conditions of fishing further north.

At the time the weather was normal, and there was no indication as to an approaching storm. They arrived at Breivik Fjord about 11.30 a.m., and anchored, as on many previous occasions, about half a mile from the shore, having always found that a safe anchorage.

The weather when the trawler arrived was still good and the glass steady. At about 1.45 p.m. on 6th November a small boat, manned by three men, put off from the shore for the purpose of taking him ashore. He persuaded his two passengers (spare hands) to accompany him so that they could see the conditions ashore while he was transacting his business.

After securing the information he required he and the two passengers went to a friend's house for some coffee. Noticing that the wind was freshening he set off to the pier, so as to return to his ship, at about 4 p.m. In less than ten minutes there was a gale blowing and the wind had changed to the westward.

"I could not get anyone to risk taking me off to the *Golden Deeps*," he said, "so I borrowed a lamp and Morsed to the ship. I could not get a reply, but kept continuously sending the message 'Get out.' I knew that if the second hand saw my message he would understand to heave the anchor and proceed to sea.

"Being dark, I could not see any one on board the ship, but I could tell from the position of the ship's lights that she had swung broadside to the wind and was driving towards the shore. In about five minutes' time I saw by the position of the ship's lights that she was heeling over, and judged that she had struck the rocks. At the same time a red rocket was sent up from the ship. The vessel again heeled over heavily to starboard, and then all the lights went out.

"With a party of villagers I immediately proceeded to the scene of the disaster, which was about one and a half miles away, but owing to the nature of the rocky ground and weather it took us about two hours before we got near where the ship had struck.

"People in farmhouses close at hand had arrived and had tried to render assistance before we put in an appearance. Owing to the darkness and the heavy surf we were powerless to render any assistance, and the majority of us stood by until daylight, when I and others manned a boat and put off from the pier and searched the water in the vicinity of the wreckage, the weather now having moderated. There was no sign of the *Golden Deeps*, the local fishermen telling me the ship had sunk in eleven fathoms of water and about fifty fathoms from the shore. Eight bodies were recovered on shore. We found three floating in the water. All the bodies had life-belts on.

"I cannot advance any opinion as to the cause of the disaster," added Skipper Rogers. "Before going ashore I told the mate, whose watch it was on deck, to keep a good look-out and to blow the ship's whistle should the wind freshen, but I never heard any whistle."

Evidence was also given by Valentine Baker, who said he joined the *Golden Deeps* as a passenger and described how he and Reginald Beales went ashore with the Skipper. The latter had some business to transact, and he and Beales went ashore to 'stretch their legs.' The owner of the village store invited them to have a cup of coffee, and after about two hours ashore they made a move to the pier. On reaching the pier they found the wind had reached gale force and that no one would risk manning the boat. The force of the wind was so strong that he and Beales were blown off their feet, and they were assisted back to the store-owner's house, where they remained until the return of Skipper Rogers and the rescue party the next day.

$$\bullet \qquad \bullet \qquad \bullet \qquad \bullet \qquad \bullet \qquad \bullet$$

Next take the case of the *Lochard*. This trawler was fishing off the North Cape of Iceland, the Skipper towing on in the teeth of terrific gales, battling to make a living. But at last the weather became so bad that he was forced to run into a place called Derry Fjord for shelter. There he lay for several days kicking his heels in idleness, waiting for the storm to abate.

But the storm still raged outside, and although lie was warned that there was also ice about, he decided to risk it, and sailed out again.

No man has ever seen him since. Not one single message came over the air.

Not long afterwards the trawler *Merrivale*, bound for the Faroe fishing grounds, encountered heavy weather in thick fog, and was driven on to the deadly Skerries, those guardian devils of 'Hell's Gate'-the Pentland Firth. All hands were lost.

Next the *Picador*. She was racing home from the White Sea, her fish-holds crammed with prime fish, her Skipper all-out to catch a Monday's market. The weather was fine and clear as she entered the North Sea. Then her wireless hummed.

The owners in Grimsby wired the Skipper to fetch a later market, as prices were bad. So he eased up and fog came down. Had he not received that fatal message it is long odds he would have got safely home. In the thick of the fog the little vessel was run down by an oil tanker and another victim was added to the long toll of disasters.

When we are homeward bound, and nearing the Humber, we always send wireless messages to our wives and sweethearts, telling them when to expect our arrival. The womenfolk then gather at a place called 'the corner,' a sheltered spot near the docks, to welcome us home. They wait a long time, some of these brave lasses, many even unto eternity.

The *Edgar Wallace*, called after the famous writer, pranced up the Humber not long ago, full of fish and optimism, for the market stood at peak.

The usual messages had been sent out, and the lasses were already at 'the corner.' Then the fog came down, when the unlucky crew were practically within sight of their own doorsteps; she struck a sandbank, and the terrific flow of the tide turned the little ship completely over. All hands were lost with the exception of two, who were picked up after swimming for an hour in the ice-cold water.

Then we have what are called 'minor casualties.' The 'doors' and great steel warps claim many victims every year, and I have seen a man's head completely severed from his neck with a breaking warp, so swift and clean that the headless body actually walked a few yards with the life blood spurting from the torn stump of neck like a stream.

A brand new ship, the *Berkshire*, had a bollard torn clean out of the deck by a breaking warp, so tremendous was the strain. The net had come fast on some larger obstruction than usual, and the curling wire, lashing like a great gigantic snake cut two men clean in half, and horribly mutilated two others, Harold Senior and Albert Steele.

Not long ago, Charles Spence, Mate of the *Stoke City* was jammed on the ship's side by one of the trawl doors as it was being hauled in, and almost flattened to pulp.

On the same vessel, one of the revolving bollards, which swing from the top of the gallows, came fast, the bollard came down, breaking the steep warp, and cut the body of a deckie, Arthur Burrows, clean in two halves, as easy as a knife severs cheese.

Again, the trawler *Mars* ran ashore at Stromness, Pentland Firth, and eight men clambered to the whaleback to pull a warp aboard from another trawler which had dashed to the rescue. A second after the tow rope had been secured and it looked as if the men would be towed to safety, a tremendous sea swept them overboard, and only one was saved.

On the trawler *Simpson*, a deckie named Davis was caught by a kink in the warp as the net was being heaved aboard. The wire fastened round his wrist and whisked him to the masthead, where he hung like a bag of coal. Several men scrambled up the rigging to release him, but before they could reach him Davis crashed to the deck. Result: two broken legs, two broken arms, four fractured ribs, and three fingers torn off.

Aboard my own ship, on one voyage, one of my trimmers had his hand jammed in the revolving winch. He was wearing gloves at the time, and after his hand was released, he pulled the glove off the damaged hand and we observed that three fingers had been torn off from the knuckles.

"Look, Skipper," he said to me quite calmly, holding up his torn hand. "Why, I've lost three fingers!" He gazed round for a moment, looking for the missing digits, and then he turned up the glove and gave it a shake. Out dropped the three fingers, and immediately he saw them he crashed to the deck in a dead faint.

It only remains for me to add that every third trawlerman fishing these waters is minus one finger, or more, and that one in ten of those now ashore is short of a limb or two.

So much for our 'minor casualties.'

But let me swing back to shipwreck, and the epic story of a rescue, which, in my humble opinion, deserves foremost place of honour of all the daring deeds performed by my comrades of the Northern Trawl.

On Friday, the 13th November, 1931, the trawler *Howe* of Grimsby, sailed down the Humber commanded by a pal of mine, Skipper George McGregor, known as 'Russian George' to all his friends.

The superstitious will note both the day and the date. His destination was Bear Island, a small, isolated rock about ten miles long by eight across, lying well inside the Arctic Circle, in latitude 750 N, about 1,500 miles north of the Humber.

In winter it is either ice or fog-bound, or wrapped in the eternal blanket of the Arctic night, with the exception of a grey daylight between ten in the morning and noon, and swept everlastingly with Atlantic gales, which veer round from east to west without warning, bringing in their train blizzard, black squall, and 40° of frost according to the direction of the wind.

On the west side the jagged cliffs rise sheer from the water's edge to several hundred feet in places, with the highest point, Mount Misery, well-named, 1,600 feet above sea level.

Inland, the island is as barren and desolate as its sea-board. Intersected with swamps, quicksands, and gigantic volcanic boulders, although only eight miles across from east to west, it is practically impassable on foot. This fact should be well borne in mind.

It belongs to Norway, and in 1931 four people lived ashore, two Norwegians, Thorlaf Johansen and Egil Lindberg, the operators in charge of the wireless station, with their wives.

There is no light or warning beacon on any part of the shore-line, and to approach the island in winter requires the courage of a lion at any time. We curse it long and often, but still we go there because the fish are there in millions in winter.

That's our job.

About 2.30 a.m., 19th November, 'Russian George' went below from the bridge, leaving the Mate in charge of his watch. There was a strong sou'westerly wind at the time with heavy swell, but visibility was good, and there was neither land nor ships in sight.

Earlier in the evening the Skipper had set a course which he expected would bring him about ten miles sou'east of Cape Bull of Bear Island towards daybreak, allowing sufficient margin (or so he thought) for magnetic compass variation, but not for abnormal attraction.

At 3.10 a.m. the Mate was relieved by the Third Hand, and before going off watch the officer entered the Skipper's cabin and reported 'All clear !'

"No sign of land?" asked George.

"Not yet, Skipper !" the Mate answered, and then asked : "Shall I ship the pound boards ready for fishing?"

"No. We'll wait till we get in touch with several of the other vessels at the island," said George.

The *Howe* was doomed never to fish again.

At 3.45 a.m. on Thursday, 19th November, 1931', whilst George was preparing to go on the bridge, he was suddenly startled by the frantic yell of the Bo'sun overhead, followed by the clang of the engine telegraph. He rushed on the bridge as the ship crashed on a hidden blinder, and dead ahead, barely 500 yards away, he saw the white breakers swirling high on the sinister cliffs of Bear Island.

A few minutes later wind and tide hurled her on the rocks.

Her stem leapt high in the air as she struck. She quivered and shuddered for a moment, then heeled to port.

Down, down, her stern submerged to the bridge and swinging like a pendulum, her funnel almost flat on the water, the breakers crashing across peak and foredeck, and thudding with the force of giant battering-rams against her helpless hulk.

Her stem was fast jammed between two hidden blinders, but her stern was free, the on-rushing waves, of tidal force, alternately picking her up on the swell and crashing her down on the rocks.

Seconds before she struck her crew had fought their way to the wheelhouse, now the only place not under water with the exception of the masts.

Fourteen men had clawed their way into a space about ten feet square, now heeling at an angle of forty-five degrees, and swinging like a clock pendulum, and immediately she struck a huge sea crashed against the bridge, smashing every pane of glass on the structure, exposing the unfortunate men to the full force of wind and lashing spray.

The time was 4 a.m. Thursday, and it seemed only a question of hours before the merciless breakers would pound her into a twisted mass of shapeless iron.

Even if she held overnight, the men were without food, and practically without shelter, and as long as the wind held to the nor'west, blowing hard against the land on the side of the island where they were ashore, no other vessel could dare to approach that deadly coast-line, and escape the same fate as their own.

There was only one chance of salvation…a million to one against.

The stem of the ship was hard up on the rocks at the bottom of the towering cliffs. It would be easy to throw a life-line and breeches-buoy from the top down on to the bridge and haul the men up the cliff-side one by one. 'Russian George' had sent out a call for help immediately he struck, and already over thirty vessels, mostly from Hull and Grimsby, were racing to the rescue. But these ships would make direct for his position, on the windward side of the island.

They must be stopped.

His wireless batteries were fast running down, but with practically the last spark he wirelessed "Rescue impossible this side. Suggest you make for leeside. Send shore party with breech buoy. Hard up on cliffs four miles west of Bull."

Skipper George did not know that Bear Island was practically impassable overland in summer daylight. In winter darkness only the stoutest hearts would ever dare to leave the coast-line leeward.

The rescuers would have to face eight miles of quicksands and swamps, loose, jagged boulders and hidden crevices, where no hand-compass would guide them, or light show the way, and with a howling gale of wind blowing face on.

There seemed no hope for the crew of the *Howe*.

The two Norwegian wireless operators were the first to attempt a land rescue. Immediately they received the last message of the *Howe*, they at once set off across the island armed with breeches buoy and electric hand lamps. They struggled on gallantly, risking death or a broken limb at every yard, and well-nigh frozen alive with the biting wind. After battling for about eight hours they were forced to give in, and were fortunate to get back to the wireless station alive. We learnt afterwards that they actually reached the opposite coastline but were unable to find the *Howe* in the darkness. No lights would be showing on the vessel by this time, as her batteries would have given out long since.

Meanwhile the Grimsby trawler *Elf King*, with young Skipper Drinkall aboard, was ploughing her way to leeward of the island. Not yet thirty, it was Drinkall's first trip in command. Desperately anxious to make good he was racing home for market, his fish holds full, when he picked up the last message of the *Howe*. He was 1,500 miles from the Humber, and had left his run home to the last possible minute.

Every hour's delay meant that his fish would deteriorate in quality, and fetch so much less on the market. But he did not hesitate for one split second.

Here is an exact copy of his wirelessed reply to the *Howe*.

"Elf King to Howe...are coming along right now...30 miles E.S.E. your position...Had just started for home...We'll take you with us...Keep smiling!"

From this point we'll allow Skipper Ernest Drinkall to finish this story. It has never before appeared in print and it is only by a great deal of persuasion that I have got him to speak now.

He says:

"I arrived off the east side of Bear Island about 8 a.m. on Thursday, 19th November. The *Howe* had then been ashore about five hours. The *Pennine*, a Hull trawler, had arrived ahead of me and I ran alongside and dropped anchor. Her Skipper informed me that he had already landed a party, and I also heard that the two Norwegians had gone several hours before. The weather was moderating, but it was still pitch black, and bitterly cold. I at once called for volunteers and sent off a shore party of six of my crew, headed by the Mate, about 9 a.m.

"Meanwhile, other ships were arriving and each at once, about twenty-five of them, landed parties until, towards noon, there were over 100 men trying to force a passage across the island. Our thoughts, of course, were with those poor devils on the *Howe*, and we knew that if the temperature fell they would die of exposure long before help could reach them.

"About 3 p.m. we heard that the wireless operators had turned back, and when our own men started filtering back, their boots absolutely worn off their feet with the rocks, and completely exhausted, I began to feel a little desperate.

"By this time there was at least thirty ships riding at anchor, and we looked like a miniature town.

"A number of skippers had boarded the *Cape Spartivento*, a Hull trawler, and I went aboard also and suggested we form a party composed entirely of skippers. But this was turned down, rightly, I suppose, the older men saying we had no right to leave our ships.

"Early next morning, Friday the 20th, when my own party returned, I felt that I had to do something for my pals on the *Howe*. They'd been on that ship now for thirty hours, and must be in a terrible plight.

"Meanwhile, my own fish wasn't improving, and as my dynamo was spinning round burning up fuel, I was likely to run short of coal unless I could get away soon.

"I thought at first of trying the weather side and a rescue from seawards, but the *Imperialist*, who was standing by the *Howe*, had wirelessed across that nothing possible could be done from that side until the gale moderated.

"The *Imperialist* also informed us that they had seen a flare coming from the bridge of the *Howe*, which meant that at least some of the crew were still alive. By this time all the shore parties had returned, all in a state of complete exhaustion, having failed to cross the island.

"About 6 a.m. on the Saturday morning I called for volunteers from all ships, and formed a party of eleven.

"We landed ashore loaded with provisions, sixty fathoms of buoy line, a buoy, and two dan buoy lights, and made for the wireless station.

One of the operators, Egil Lindberg, although he had already been across the island and his feet were raw and bandaged, at once volunteered to show us the best way across. The men on the *Howe* had now been on that ship two days and nights, and I felt that everything depended on my party.

"It was 8 a.m. on Saturday when we set off and our object was to reach the other side if possible before noon so as to take advantage of what daylight there was. I was convinced 'Russian George' had mistaken his position, and we might miss the *Howe* in the darkness, even if we did get near her. The lights of the dan buoy only gave out the faintest glimmer, and would only last a certain time.

"Before I left the wireless station, I said to the other operator, who could speak English: 'Inform my ship by wireless that if I can't reach the *Howe* before dark, I shall remain on the island all night. I'm not coming back without the *Howe's* crew.'

"Before we had gone far we began to sink in the quicksands, and after about an hour several of my party became exhausted.

'Those of you who can't keep up, go back,' I told them, and one by one they dropped down deadbeat. We others pushed on, but towards late afternoon only four of us were left, the Norwegian, one of my trimmers, the bosun of the *Spartivento*, and myself.

"The darkness was coming on again, but we struggled on, sometimes sinking up to our waists in a white, sticky clay that clung like putty, at others splashing blindly through sopping marshes, or falling over rocks, and none of us certain whether we were making in the right direction or not.

"We had long since dumped the provisions, and were now dragging only the rescue gear.

"Early on Sunday morning we reached the opposite coast, and began to feel our way along the cliff-tops, although we were knocked off our feet again and again by the wind.

"The men had now been on the *Howe* for close on seventy hours, and we knew we must hurry on if we were to find any alive.

"It was almost impossible to see a yard ahead, but down below we could see the white surge of the breakers, and out at sea the lights of several trawlers crawling along the coast.

Late that night, when we were all sitting in a silent circle on that Godforsaken, barren rock, at our last gasp, we suddenly saw several lights swinging towards us. Another party had won through with provisions. They had only corned beef, bread, and cold tea, but by heavens! that bully beef went down better than all the turkey I have ever tasted. The return journey, although less than eight miles, took us fourteen hours, and by the time we reached our ships my rescue party had been out for twenty-four hours, the longest day I have ever spent in my life."

That's the end of Skipper Drinkall's personal description of that thrilling adventure, but it's not quite the end of the story.

Every man who took part in that gallant rescue received appropriate recognition, including the two Norwegians. The late King was pleased to shake the hand of Skipper Drinkall, and the Board of Trade presented him with a handsome piece of plate.

But his fish was sent to the manure dump, he settled in debt, and for several months Skipper Ernest Drinkall was out of a ship.

Thus are heroes rewarded. But now read how the law describes this epic story of the sea. I have never yet received one of the following documents, but they are very common down Humber way, and this one is well worthy of inclusion in my log.

· · · · · ·

BY THIS PUBLIC INSTRUMENT OF PROTEST
be it known and made manifest that on the 2nd day of December One thousand nine hundred and thirty-one personally appeared before me HAROLD MOUNTAIN Notary Public by Royal Authority duly admitted and sworn and practising at Great Grimsby in the County of Lincoln in the United Kingdom of Great Britain and Northern Ireland GEORGE McGREGOR Skipper of the steam trawler "*HOWE*" Official Number 160982 registered as a fishing vessel at the Port of Grimsby who did duly
and solemnly declare and state as follows that is to say:-

1. THAT he and the rest of the crew of fifteen hands of the said vessel set sail in her from Grimsby on the thirteenth day of November last bound on a fishing voyage to the vicinity of Bear Island the vessel then being tight, staunch and strong, well manned, victualled and sound and in every respect fit to perform her said intended voyage.

2. THAT they continued on their voyage and on Tuesday the seventeenth day of November last at about 7.30 a.m. when the Lofoten Islands bore East from the vessel and approximately twenty miles distant the course was changed and the log re-set. The course set from that position was north-east by north half north which course he estimated would bring him after steaming four hundred and thirty miles to the fishing grounds in a position about ten miles south-east of Cape Bull of Bear Island.

3. THAT they proceeded on the north-east by north half north course and on Wednesday the eighteenth day of November last the log was read at 12 noon and showed two hundred and eighty-five miles. It was again read at 12 midnight when it showed four hundred and six miles. There was a

strong wind from the southwest with heavy swell and the visibility very good with bright moonlight. At frequent intervals as was his invariable custom on approaching close to land he went on the bridge to assure himself that everything was in order. He went below from the bridge at 2.30 a.m. leaving the Mate in charge of his watch. The on-coming watch was called at 3 a.m. and the Mate's watch was relieved at 3.10 a.m. when the Mate came into his cabin and reported "All clear" and that there was neither land nor ships in sight and that the visibility continued to be very good. The Mate asked him if he required him to get the pound boards shipped ready for fishing. He replied that he did not want this doing until other fishing vessels were sighted and that he should go on the bridge himself in half an hour. The Mate then left the cabin, it was 3.20 a.m.

4. THAT at about 3.45 a.m. whilst he was preparing to go on the bridge the ship suddenly crashed on to some obstacle which afterward proved to be a reef. He rushed on to the bridge and saw cliffs plainly ahead at a distance he judged to be about half a mile. The telegraph had been put on full speed astern by the Third Hand who was on watch and who was, he then found, the only man on the bridge. The engines were going full speed astern but the vessel was still making considerable headway with the large swell from aft and was bumping badly. The Chief Engineer reported that the vessel was filling rapidly. He ordered engines to be stopped and boiler valves to be opened, and instructed the Wireless

Operator to send out distress signals; also he sent up distress rockets and showed flares. By this time the vessel had drifted in to within forty yards of the cliff and was hard aground and almost full of water in all compartments. The vessel had been holed badly in many places.

5. THAT the crew and this Appearer left the vessel after two and a half days being rescued by a shore party, as the vessels which answered their distress signals could not approach them to render assistance on account of the heavy swell breaking over the reef where the vessel first struck.

7. THAT this Appearer left for Grimsby aforesaid on the twenty-second day of November last because it was evident to him that in the circumstances and position of the said vessel there was no hope of salving either the said vessel or any of its gear~

WHEREFORE this Appearer declares to protest and I the said Notary at his request do also protest against stranding striking strong winds and heavy seas facts incident and occurrences aforesaid and for all and every loss cost detriment damage and expense that has arisen or can or may arise therefrom to the end that the same may be borne and sustained by those to whom the right it doth can or may appertain.

I, GEORGE McGREGOR do solemnly and sincerely declare that the foregoing statement is correct and contains a true account of the facts and circumstances and I make this solemn declaration conscientiously believing the same to be true and by virtue of the provisions of the Statutory Declarations Act I 835.

(Sgd.) GEORGE McGREGOR.

DECLARED and PROTESTED in due form of law at Great Grimsby aforesaid this second day of December One thousand nine hundred and thirty-one.

Stamp.

One shilling.

HAROLD MOUNTAIN, Notary Public, GREAT GRIMSBY, England.

And so say all of us.

Chapter 6

THE BRATS

Aboard S.T. Arsenal.
Trawling Lat. 62° 20" N. Long 41° 25" W.

O ld Feathery's Hell's Legions unleashed!
We're steaming slap into the teeth of nor '-westerly gale this
morning. The ruddy seas are as high as the shore mountains, four
miles off the starboard beam.

The farther these mountains are astern the better I'll like it. That's
why we're steaming for the wideopen spaces. Give this 'Highbury Lass'
plenty sea room an' she'll snort defiance in the face of a typhoon. But
she don't like mountains, unless they green and soft, like the ones she's
climbing now.

Up, you beauty, up and over! Up the *Arsenal*. This is the time to see
this girl in action, when Old Feathery's doing his darnedest.

Like most of her sisters she was built on Tyne, and I reckon the
Geordies know their job.

Run an eye over her, and never mind her rust and grime. She's built
for service', hard, ceaseless, relentless graft, and not for looks.

Fog, blizzard, ice, hurricane, calm or storm, or foul, they all come
alike to her, and the harder blows the better she like's it.

Every riveted plate in this ocean pirate gives impression of power,
strength, defiance.

Ugly! Look at her lines and marvel!

The whaleback towers for'ard, set above a stem sharp as a two-edged
sword; amidships, her lines curve gracefully down, the rails low in the
water, with the bridge, high, narrow, a square tower of welded steel, rising
dead centre; aft, the line again curves upwards, forming almost a half-
circle ending in a stern, broad, square, like a cruiser's; and she's steel, the
entire hulk, even the masts, from stem to keelson.

Aye, we trawlermen are proud of our ships, and grateful to our shore pals on Tyneside. They know what we've got to face sometimes, and even although only 150 registered tons and the same number of feet in length, our little vessels will live in a sea that'd sink a lifeboat.

Swish! Watch her razor snout sweep the seas aside'. Crash ! A great, green comber smashes aboard.

Toss! And she's dry as a bone. Come on, Old Feathery! Who cares a damn about you! Swish!

Crash ! Toss

Sometimes a wave sneaks in amidships, and Old Feathery thinks he's got her. Roll! Down, down she goes until her funnel's almost flat on the water. Shake! and up she comes again still dry as a bone.

That's why she curves low in the centre. Sometimes a wave sweeps clean over the whaleback and crashes against the bridge, but that structure's of welded steel. Sometimes a following sea sweeps aft, but that stern is broad, and flat, low in the water, like a raft. In the trough, sometimes a sea smashes down on the peak before she has time to rise, but her nose is shaped like the back of a whale, and she tosses it off with one little shake of the stem.

Aye, I reckon the designers know their job, and we mustn't forget it when we think of fish. Let's give her a pat all to herself she deserves full mention in this log, she and her designers, and England ought to be proud of these sturdy little ocean plungers. Even the scrub (the foreigner) has copied her design, rivet by rivet, and they are buying her sisters wholesale from the Tyne. Aye, and they'll come in useful if another war happens along, as they did in the past. So build another thousand, I Say, there's plenty of men to handle them down Humber way.

But jump on the bridge beside me. The gallant *Stoke City* is just abeam. I can only see the tip of her masts as she wallows in the trough.

"This weather's a fair cow, isn't it, Albert?"

Tom Evans, her skipper, addresses me over the radiophone. I can't answer back until he switches over to me.

"A bloody cow, Albert," he repeats. Tom often repeats himself over the 'phone. We all do that, strangely enough. I suppose it gives us time to think of the next sentence. "But I'm sticking…I'm sticking, Albert, and damn old Feathery. Yow. Pulled up thirty baskets last haul, the cod-end busted, and I lost the bloody lot…Yow! And they wonder why skippers swear and eat deckies, Albert. Had a yarn with *Bernard Shaw* this morning. He split his bloody belly, last dip. Yow! Mae West wiggin'.

Mae jumped in to tell me *Larwood* and *Bradman* off to the old Ale town. Yow! Don's beat bodyline by about 200. Is that the *Spurs* off your starboard quarter, Albert?

"Here's some markets just come through, Albert. *Leicester City*

Men say these waters are hunted. They speak of a ghost ship
that comes gliding abeam out of fog and blizzard.

MR. WILLIAM ("Bull Brack") BRACKENBURY,
Manager and first salesman of Consolidated Fisheries Ltd.

Up shot a rocket, and there was the stem of the *Howe* almost
beneath us, nearly 100 feet below

"THE ARSENAL TEAM"

Note the 'football,' or one of the ponderous steel bobbins on the right of the picture

The fish somersaults high in the air and lands with a squelchy
thud in the washing pounds on the opposite side

Bill Martin, Skipper of the Trawler *King Stephen*, encountered the Zepp lying
disabled on the water about sixty miles east of Grimsby

SIR JOHN MARSDEN, BART.
Chairman, Consolidated Fisheries Ltd.

Skipper Hutchinson's present ship, S.T. *Arsenal*

Manchester City

landed 2,000 baskets Friday, made £1,110...*Blackburn Rovers* 1,900 baskets, made £970.

How much have you got in, Albert? I've got about 1,200 baskets below, 200 cats, 150 ducks, and about 50 flats. I expect I shall steam for next Wednesday's market! Yow! When are you stowing-up, Albert?

I've finished! Over to you, Albert! Over!"

Thus we help one another over the 'phone. I might have missed the latest market reports, but Tom passes them on.

This helps me to gauge the market, and thus guides me when to 'stow-up' and steam home with my own catch.

We're never anxious to get home when prices are low, but even with a lesser catch it pays to steam for home on a rising market.

"*Bernard Shaw* split his belly last dip!"

Any one ashore idly turning the knobs of a wireless set and hearing those words might get a bit of a shock, but it simply means that the trawler named after the famous Irishman had the belly of the net torn during fishing operations, and "Don beat Bodyline by about 200," tells me that both vessels are steaming home, the *Larwood* with 200 less baskets of fish aboard than the *Bradman*.

'Mae' West is the Skipper of the *Spurs*, towing to our starboard. We call him 'Mae' because of his surname, and he has been listening to our conversation. Hence, he jumped in' with the information about the *Larwood* and the *Bradman*.

I reply

"*Arsenal... Stoke City...* Hello! Hello! Hello! ... Good morning, Tom! ...Yes, got you okay posh! Aye, we're having a basinful this trip, Tom. Wouldn't be so bad if Old Feathery'd give us just a bit of a break. 20 baskets all night! Yow! Came fast at midnight. Both wings split! Had a helofa job getting her round to windward. I was afraid she would sit on her gear and foul the propeller. Yow! Touch and go, Tom, touch and go! But I'm stickin'! The brats have been on deck all night mending the port trawl.

Curse! Yow! Yes, it's the old *Spurs* behind! He's stickin'! I've got 1,300 baskets, Tom. Market seems to be rising a bit! Aye, you're steaming for Wednesday, Tom! Reckon I'll stow her up for Thursday or Friday! Yow! I'm dipping her in again, Tom. Aye, I'll risk another haul! I've finished. Don't come back. I've gone! Over!"

Aye, it's blowing like the Wrath of God this morning. Most of the other ships have packed up.

"I'm giving the lads a break. I'm laying!"

I heard a Skipper say that over the 'phone just now. Watch the gaffers give him a break when he gets home-breaking ice on the pontoon. Aye, wi' clogs on-and nobs.

No, as I have said before, there's little room for sentiment in this game.

Hard! Relentless! Savage! That's what it is-always.

Only one thing counts-fish. If the fish are coming steady-40, 50, 6o baskets a haul, and no splits, then my brats can have a rodger between each haul, and they know it.

The Skipper can't, not while the trawl's on the bottom. But that reminds me. I must introduce you to the *Arsenal* team-my team, and if our shore team at Highbury in London would like to challenge us to a game of football we'll take them on, providing they're prepared to gut and clean a big tiger cat-fish for every goal they score against us. Up the *Arsenal* !

I have eighteen men ... brats ...deckies, in my team, and if there are eighteen tougher guys in Chicago I'll eat raw Sprags.

My brats wallow in blood and drink about ten gallons of salt water every day, and if any Dago can handle a knife quicker than they can I'd like the gentleman to step into my fish pounds. There's always a job aboard this ship for a fellow that likes blood and salt water, and can handle a knife, and can do without that bucket I mentioned earlier on.

Without exaggeration these fellows are living the most savage, the most cruel, the hardest, and most dangerous life on God's earth. Every hour of their lives they are wallowing up to their necks in blood, offal, and water, tearing the guts out of squirming, living fish . . . blue cats, tiger cats, six feet long with savage jaws, and teeth that can sheer a sea-boot easier than a knife cuts butter, halibut, twice as big as themselves, cod weighing fifteen stone, haddocks, coalies, soldiers, flats, and an occasional shark. We caught a shark once which weighed over three tons.

The fish pounds, square, boarded compartments each large enough to take half a ton of fish, are on the for'ard, or well deck, six pounds on each side of the ship. The fish are gutted on one side, and cleaned on the other.

When the trawl is hauled out of the water the cod-end, or apex of the net, where all the fish congregate, is grappled by a gilson hook and heaved high inboard over the pounds. The cod-end is laced by a rope and when this is undone the fish drop into the pounds. That looks dead easy on paper.

Try and imagine what it means in blizzard and gale with the ship climbing mountains, both rails alternatively deep under water, seas and spray lashing aboard, and the temperature 40° below zero.

I've seen salt spray turn into thin, solid sheets of ice as soon as it hit the deck, scattering splinters keen as broken, jagged glass, cutting the men's faces to ribbons. Exaggeration! Is it?

The latest ships carry costly plant and special hot-water hoses to thaw the ice-spray, which can convert a ship literally into an iceberg within hours. Many a trawler has turned turtle down North because of the weight of ice, which has formed overnight on her sides, riggings, and decks. They talk to us one minute over the 'air,' the next silence.

That's all

Winter or summer, one of the deckies must crawl beneath that swaying swagbag, to loosen the rope securing the cod-end. He disappears from sight once he enters the arc of the streaming waterfall of ice-cold water which gushes out of the net. Imagine a shower bath in a blizzard with the temperature forty below?

That bag may hold several tons of struggling, writhing fish, and he must leap for his life when the great maw opens and the fish crash out.

That also looks easy on paper. Put a pair of skates on your feet and try chasing a balloon on a revolving skating rink, with someone splashing a fire-hose of ice-cold water in your face.

Men have misjudged the ship's roll by the barest fraction of a second only when untying that bag. That split second was the dividing line between life and death. Even the back of an elephant would not stand the strain of two tons of fish crashing a-top.

Look down into my fish pounds from the height of my bridge. Thrills! This is men's work. Last haul I landed two tons of fish, a record for the trip. My pounds are full to the brim, each five feet deep by ten feet square. The brats are up to the waistline, legs completely hidden in those struggling, squirming heaps of fighting fish, the water dripping in cascades from their gleaming oilskins.

A haul of fish is gutted and cleaned immediately it leaves the water, and not allowed to remain on deck one minute longer than necessary. A good crew of ten deckies will gut, clean, and ice a ton of fish in an hour. They work like savages-fiends, maddened with blood-lust, especially in winter, when death stalks that lurching, storm-washed deck. Every minute saved means a minute less on that death trap when the seas are crashing aboard.

Watch the knives flash! Rip! A lightning ten-inch slash, and the pulsating entrails of a six-foot writhing cod bursts through the gleaming belly. Slash! A twist of the wrist and the liver falls into a basket. Rip!... and the unwanted offal is torn out and thrown on deck. Still grasping the struggling fish, fighting in its death throes, the deckies' shoulders swing back, like a Highlander tossing the caber. He heaves, the fish somersaults high in the air and lands with a squelshy thud in the washing pounds on the opposite side of the ship.

Rip! . . Splash! . . Heave! . . Thud!

Soon the men's feet are ankle deep in offal, the decks streaming red with blood, and no shore shambles can look more ghastly.

Aye, a hard, savage life, cruel, relentless, ferocious. These fish are still alive when the guts are torn from them, they live on in the washing pound even when disembowelled, for a space, and I often wonder if they can feel as we can feel. Still, you want fish, and there's no other way.

Let me say this about the lads, although it looks like a pat on the back for myself. . . . They never tire, never complain. Fog, rain, wind, storm, blizzard, black-squall, ice, broken head-lines, split nets, cuts, bruises, bites, water, water up to their necks, a rolling, lurching, heaving vessel which does everything except turn upside down, hard, ceaseless, heartbreaking graft, they leap to their work with song or curse, according to the mood, and the harder it blows the louder they curse, and when they forget to rave and swear their laughter and song is just as loud. That's not all; every deckie sailing these waters faces death every hour of his life in winter, and nearly every one of my crew has been concerned in the rescue, and the attempted rescue, of others, not once but a hundred times, against odds and under conditions which I defy any pen to describe.

Every single fish is gutted, cleaned, and packed singly in layers on the ice shelves between decks, a high work of art and the responsibility of the Mate. Refrigeration has proved unsuccessful, and we find that our old method ensures that the fish arrives at the market firm and hard and as fresh as when it is caught. It also keeps longer after it is unpacked.

But now I must tell you something about our life aboard.

Steaming to and fro to our grounds generally occupies from eight to ten days each trip according to the weather, and we then revert to the routine of a merchant ship. Between watches the brats yarn, read, and listen-in to the wireless.

They like lowbrow stuff with plenty of gagging, and the Saturday night 'Music Hall' always draws a few to the wheelhouse, where the loud-speaker is located. Operas and classical music-"Haw! Haw Crap!" they call that stuff-starts them scrapping.

Books! A lot of nice people send us books. The brats like blood, red-raw gangster stuff, and in the picture line they like legs…photographs of female cinema stars.

Aye, blood and legs! Seems they don't get enough of blood, and yet if you were to set a mob of thugs against my brats reckon the gangsters'd look like ewe lambs in comparison.

Take Alex Baines for instance one of my deckies. This ewe lamb has the strength of three men and the shoulders of a bullock. He has been shipwrecked thrice, concerned in over thirty rescues, and has met with every accident possible on a trawler, and that's saying a mouthful. He has also had umpteen scraps with the bogey-man, and on one ship his Skipper actually attacked the gun-boat, laid out three of the officers, later to be captured and sentenced to six years imprisonment in Iceland.

But, bless me, if you were to tell Alex he was a tough guy he'd probably drop down dead with surprise.

Aye, he's a tough guy all right. Yow!

Then there's Abe Sampson, my Mate. Abe carries a Skipper's ticket, and what he can't do with a trawl net isn't worth worrying about. As a lad, he sailed as a deckie in the North Sea during the War, and he has a yarn to tell about a certain Zeppelin, the Z17, which set the whole world yapping in February, 1916.

Bill Martin, Skipper of the Trawler *King Stephen* encountered the Zepp lying disabled on the water about sixty miles east of Grimsby. The German crew numbered thirty and they were probably armed.

Skipper Martin's crew numbered ten, unarmed. The Zepp was slowly sinking and the German Commander begged Skipper Martin to take them off. But the risk was too great. Martin refused, and steamed for Grimsby, at once reporting the matter to the Admiralty. Destroyers raced to the spot indicated, but nothing more was ever seen or heard of either the Zepp or the crew.

The Germans sent three submarines to revenge that Zepp, and laid doggo for three months near the Humber until they finally captured the *King Stephen*. The crew were sent to the salt mines, and Abe's cousin had his leg broken by the mob when they first landed in Germany.

But another Skipper had command of the *King Stephen*, and when the Germans discovered that the man they wanted, Bill Martin, was missing, they sent secret agents to Grimsby and got him as well. Bill died suddenly and very mysteriously, and his end is still a bit of a mystery which we people in Grimsby have never quite been able to understand.

Charlie Landmore, my cook, is the most important man on the ship, and incidentally he believes in mermaids and sea serpents, especially since the coming of his baby. He once retrieved a baby mermaid from the fish pounds, or so he swears.

Unfortunately it died and he buried it at sea. Had Charlie ever landed the dead body in England it would have brought him a fortune in the show booths.

A few months back one of his skipper pals was fined £10 for swearing over the mike. The P.M.G.'s bogey-man, who listens-in to trawlermen's radio-phone conversation somewhere near Wick, got him.

Had that gentleman seen Charlie last trip swimming amongst his pots and pans, with his left ear filled with mashed potatoes and a red-hot carrot sticking in his right, when a sea washed him out of the galley, and had heard our cookie's remarks. Oh, my!

"Tut, tut, you naughty little ship!"

Charlie's brawny arms are scarred from shoulder to wrists, life-marks of a thousand scalds. Try cooking on that revolving rink with skates on I mentioned further back.

Good cooks are as rare as a middleman's charity. When we get a good 'un we lock him up in port to prevent another' crew pinching him. When we get a bad 'un, well, I reckon life becomes a little more hellish than it is at the best of times.

Charlie is old now, nigh on sixty, and beginning to think of the scrap-heap. He's sailed these seas for nearly half a century, the best cook out of Grimsby, and as long as he can stand on his feet I reckon he'll play for the *Arsenal* team.

Strangely enough, although our cooks lead a comparatively sheltered life free from the hundred-and-one dangers which the deckhands have to face, we lose more cooks than deckies at sea.

"I reckon they get fed-up, Skipper, trying to cook in a closet where the floor's nearly always where the roof ought to be, and just quietly slip over the side one night when nobody's looking." Thus said Charlie at dinner today. "I've felt like doing it many a time myself," he added quietly, and by the look in his eyes I knew he was in deadly earnest.

Big Paddy, my Chief Engineer, sitting opposite, snorted when he heard that. Paddy has sailed with me for a good many years, and we had a few rotten cooks before Charlie slung his dunnage aboard.

The big Chief hasn't forgotten them. "Slip overboard!" snarled Paddy. "By the holy jabers, we slung the spalpeens overboard," he growled.

One cook we had made delicious soup. He had a big pot in the galley, and everything left over from dinner was slung into this to make stock. One cold night, Paddy, thinking a little drop of hot soup wouldn't do him any harm, unearthed the stockpot. When the Chief removed the lid he saw a white, sticky mess, about an inch thick, adhering to the sides of the pot. Paddy thought this was fat at first, but when he looked closer he suddenly lost his appetite.

The white, sticky mess were maggots, real, live, squirming maggots . . . Yow!

"Yes, we sling the spalpeens overboard !" growled Paddy again.

Paddy does not mean one word of that. This big Irishman, six feet of brawn and whip-cord, is as tender and as gentle as a woman at heart.

Several months ago, back in dock at Grimsby, a poor little half-starved tabby kitten jumped aboard all skin and bone, and with one eyelid cut and bruised. Some swine ashore had bashed that cat. It cowered and spat at everybody that tried to touch it. Then Paddy appeared, and ever since Minnie has spent her time either in the engine-room or in the big

Irishman's bunk. She never goes anywhere else, nor will she accept food from anyone but the Chief, and now, at sea, Paddy is only concerned with two things . . . his beloved engines, and the fact that we don't carry fresh milk. Minnie won't drink the tinned variety.

We seldom spend more than thirty-six hours ashore between trips, but Paddy can still find time out of this short interval to come to the docks once a day with fresh milk for his cat, and his house lies several miles away. During the whole of the time the ship is in dock Minnie sits dejectedly outside the engine-room gangway, her eyes glued on the quay, and from this position nothing on earth can coax her until Paddy returns.

I've also got a cat, Blackie, a tom. He jumped aboard shortly after the coming of Minnie, and made pals with me. At first I thought he was a manx, but when I picked him up and stroked his stumpy little tail he screamed like a baby. Then I found blood on my hand. I'd like to have the hell fiend who chopped that kitten's tail off aboard this ship. Aye, just for one short hour.

I'm giving these cats a lot of space in this log, but believe me, they mean a lot to us.

As I've written so often before, there's little room for sentiment in this game, so perhaps these tiny, furry things keep us human. Nearly all the trawlers carry pets of some kind.

If either of our cats were to go over the side, even if I had my trawl out I'd swing round at once, aye, even if it meant fouling the propeller and losing my gear. I'd pay the damage gladly. They're worth that much to me.

But that's where Blackie will go one day, over the side. Minnie seldom comes on deck. Blackie is never off it, foul or fair.

When we shoot, Blackie is there, to see that the brats get that net out slick. When we haul, at the first sound of the whirring winch he's up on the ship's rail, as tense and eager as any aboard to see what's in the swag-bag. Then he marches to the fish pounds and stands by till the last fish is gutted and cleaned.

Sometimes he'll pounce on a squirming sprag, but he's got sense enough to keep away from the savage jaws of the blue and tiger cat-fish. Aye, Blackie gives his marine brothers and sisters a very wide berth indeed, but at least a dozen times a day a sea hurtles him into the scuppers. I whistle him on these occasions and he scurries to heel like a dog.

He is a dog; at least he behaves like one. Throw him a piece of coal, or any other article, and he'll retrieve it and bring it back. I've never seen a cat behave like him, nor one with such scant disregard for water.

He's a real tough guy, eats only raw fish, several whole haddocks as big as himself every day, heads and bones included, and drinks only water.

Between hauls he spends most of his time on the whaleback chasing gulls. The peak is generally awash, but Blackie dodges the waves as cleverly as a hoary old deck-hand, but one day he'll mistake a gannet for a gull and then . . . good-bye, Blackie.

We fishermen love the gulls and feed them; sometimes they're the only living things we see from trip to trip, apart from ourselves. The Iceland gulls never board the ship. When one does he can't take off again unless assisted by one of the men. The brats drop all work on hand when this happens and never fail to give the birds a leg-up. The Scotch gulls, on the other hand, fly aboard in hundreds when we reach the Orkneys, scrounging for grub. Charlie, the cook, has the greatest respect for the Jocks.

Homeward bound one trip, Charlie boiled a ham, the last one in the lazarette. We were going to have nice cold ham and pickles for tea that night. He cooked it to a turn, then he placed it on the engine casing aft to cool.

"I went into the galley immediately afterwards," explained Charlie, "and I remember hearing a helofa squawking overhead. I took no notice for a minute, but when the din increased until it sounded like the whistle of a thousand sirens, I thought 'Hell, these blasted Scotch gulls are after my ham.' I'd only left it on the hatch for a minute but when I dashed out all that was left was the bone, picked clean as a fish-buyer's hands-the greedy Scotch bastards!"

But still Charlie bears no malice. He often saves a few scraps for the hungry feathered Jocks.

We have scant respect for the gannets, however. These winged pirates of the Northern skies plunder the gulls' nests and slay the young from mere wanton blood-lust, and when they do alight on deck they will attack a man if molested.

I've seen one of these birds chase a deckie the whole length of a ship's deck, and they can break a limb with their powerful wings. Their keen eyes can spot fish underneath the water, and it's really a thrilling sight to see them dive. Magnificently streamlined, with outstretched wings they hover over the water from a height higher than the mast, shut their wings with a snap, shoot down with the velocity of a bullet, enter the water with scarcely a ripple, and it is said they can dive down to a depth of ten fathoms (sixty feet). Sometimes, in rough weather, they mistime their entry into the water. Result! A broken neck and a lifeless heap of fluttering feathers floating on the waves.

The gannet will swallow a 6-lb. cod at a gulp. Sometimes the head sticks out between his greedy, gaping beak and another swoops down and commences a tug-of-war. We learned things from that. We used to tie two herrings on a string to encourage the by-play.

In the old days our fish pounds were lit up at night by carbide lamps, and a favourite practice then was to slit a cod's belly, fill it with carbide, sew it up again, and toss it to master gannet. Any unfortunate bird who swallowed that morsel was very quickly minus its tail feathers. They were blown off in gusts, and the noise of the backwind—Oh!

We fishermen smile quietly when we hear folk spout about man's conquest of the air, and think of the gannet. Just as the lion is lord of the jungle, so is the gannet king of the heavens. For speed, beauty, grace, and air control, we fishermen will back him against anything that flies, and perhaps if our aviation experts were to study him they might learn things. He's equally as deadly on land or ship as he is in sea and air.

A Skipper friend of mine owned a large, black retriever dog who used to chase gulls on the whale-back. One day master gannet arrived on the peak.

The dog leaped, so did the gannet, and the retriever was minus an eye.

Aye, these are savage waters where death stalks eternally for man and beast.

Old Feathery Legs, tiger cats, and gannets! How long will Blackie survive?

When the weather is exceptionally bad Paddy secures Blackie in the engine-room, to keep Minnie company. But both are reaching the adult stage, and the other day, Blackie got fresh and Minnie clouted him, knocked him off the engine-room stairs into a barrel of oil, and now he looks as if his hair has been marcel waved. A few seconds after this happened Paddy gave me a bollo on the speaking-tube which leads from the engine-room to the bridge.

"This damned black mongrel of yours, Skipper," snapped Paddy. "I think he'll be safer on deck."

"What's the trouble, Chief?"

"Trouble! Come down and have a look at his dirty hide. I'm turning the hose pipe on him." Then Paddy entered into delicate details. "You don't expect a pedigree Irish lady to have any darned truck with a mongrel dock rat, do you?" he concluded firmly.

Poor old Blackie

Often in a storm, land birds blown out to sea seek shelter aboard, but they always die. Famished, they snap up the offal littering the deck, and the salt-impregnated food kills them.

Pigeons, on the other hand, seldom land on deck, but make straight for the roof of the bridge.

Sometimes they travel with us for weeks, taking an occasional short flight for exercise round and round the ship. They are our guests until land is sighted again, and are kept well fed with peas and fresh water every day.

One morning Blackie caught a starling, but Paddy happened to be on deck at the time, and pounced before Blackie had time to harm the bird.

Paddy marched it down into the engine-room, first securing a piece of bread and a pannikin of water from the galley. The bird pecked at the bread but refused to drink, so Paddy filled his mouth with water, placed the bird's beak inside his own, huge cavern, and kept it there until the starling was forced to drink or choke. Then he let it free, but it remained in the engine-room until we arrived back in Grimsby, eating and drinking every day. At first both Minnie and Blackie tried to catch it, but without success. Then one day, when the cats were both lying curled up asleep near Paddy's feet, the bird actually walked up to within a cat's paw of both.

Said Paddy: "I saw Blackie open his eyes and blink at the bird, but the cat was so darned amazed he looked as if he'd get up and run away for two pins. Then Minnie raised her head, and I got ready to jump, 'cause I thought sure as blazes she'll have it. But she didn't. Instead she got up, smelt it, then began to play with it. Blackie stuck his ugly black snout in then, and Minnie promptly clouted him, and for the rest of the voyage Minnie and the starling played, fed, and slept together, and if ever Blackie came near, Minnie belted him. Reckon that bird was lonely, and my Min has the makings of an Irish mother," Paddy concluded sagely.

Aye, the sea brings many strange bedfellows together, but it's a great leveller, on the little boats at least. Man's inhumanity to man is maybe merely but an expression on shore, but we still find it down North. Men can become devils out in these lonely wastes, fiends incarnate, heartless, relentless, mocking in the very face of death, cruel to all living things. But they can become very Godlike too, sometimes. Wild, hard-drinking, hard-swearing trawlermen, yarning in the quiet watches, have told me that at sea, but never on land, they sometimes 'feel' a powerful, unseen Presence, a vague something quite beyond their simple minds to define or explain, which seems to make things a little easier when human endurance has nigh reached breaking-point.

Let's leave it at that.

Chapter 7

THE ETERNAL BATTLE

Aboard S.T. Arsenal
Trawling Lat. 65° 24" N. Long 39° 26" W.

In this chapter of my narrative I append a few actual extracts from my logbook, Just to give some idea of the conditions we must face eternally to bring fish to the English market. In between, we will listen to several pals over the radio-phone, and discover if they are faring any better, or worse, than ourselves.

At the present moment I have my port trawl out, and I am fishing a ground called the Burie Deep, off the East coast of Iceland, about six miles from shore, or only three miles outside the limit line. It is winter, January, 1938, and pitch dark, with the temperature 20° below freezing point. For ten days we have been battling in the teeth of Nor'-easterly gales, with fog and blizzard in between, and although we are hard on the coast-line we haven't seen blink or sign of land since leaving Grimsby.

If we could peer far below the keel of my prancing ship, down to the ocean bottom, we would discover that the Burie Deep is a deep valley between two marine mountains standing very close together in places. The valley is roughly about thirty miles long, varying in width from one to six miles, and in depth from one hundred to one hundred and twenty fathoms. Multiply the latter by six and you get the number of feet.

The 'flats'-that is where the bottom is fairly even and free from 'nails,' the term we apply to rocks and wreckage and other obstructions which tear our nets (we apply other names)-varies from thirty to ninety fathoms deep.

In the old days, as I have previously explained, we depended on the lead-line to give us our depth, but to-day one twist of the knob on the electric echometer tells us all we want to know.

Many of the younger Skippers haven't learnt to use the lead-line, hence, when the echometer konks out, as it sometimes does, they get into a helofa jam, and depend upon others, over the radio, to help them out.

My trawl is scooping the edge of a gulley, and the little red arrow indicator of my echometer is ticking over on the 100-fathom line.

The fish here are always of first-class quality firm and plump-prime hard sprags (cod), good swag, not rich and soft, as they sometimes are only a few miles away.

Alex Baines, my leading deckie, stands behind me at the wheel. His eyes are bloodshot, red-rimmed, eyes that have not known sleep for the past twenty-four hours.

We both peer ahead. The dim grey form of a trawler looms up through the ghost-like gloom. His siren blares-one long and two short blasts, which tells us he is hauling in his net. As we are towing we must give way, so we reply with two short blasts and veer to port.

"Damn him!" Hear Alex curse as he claws on the wheel. We both curse, loud and long. The other fellow has given the wrong signal. His stem swings round slap on our course.

"Hard over your helm, Alex-and damn him again !" I yell.

The net of the other trawler is fast on a 'nail.'

We can hear the roar of his winch echoing through the gloom. Had he given the correct signal-three short blasts-we would have given him a wider berth.

We came fast ourselves last haul-a bad split, but I've wrapped net round all the 'nails' on this lousy bottom.

Sometimes we go a whole trip without a split net. On other voyages we get so many damned splits that fishing is held up for days. The majority of skippers move to fresh ground on these occasions. I generally stick!

Several miles ahead of the ground where I am fishing now, lies a great rock called the Whaleback.

We will hear it mentioned presently over the 'air.'

Its surface-about 1,000 yards in circumference-shows only about six feet above the water-line, and if the waters were to roll back this extraordinary rock would take the appearance of a slender pillar rising three times the height of Nelson's column sheer from the ocean bed. It lies about twenty miles from land, and as there is no light or warning beacon this evil 'blinder' has claimed many a victim.

Two years ago the *Juliana* was fishing close to the Whaleback in fog and gale, when she struck the rock, and such was the swiftness of the disaster that her Skipper, MacAllen, a pal of mine, had not even time to send out an S.O.S.

No man is certain of her fate, but her last wirelessed position told us that she was fishing almost under the shadow of the Whaleback death trap.

But the chance of hitting 'blinders' is only one of the thousand cards which Old Feathery plays against us in this gamble. You'll discover a few more before this chapter concludes.

Last Christmas I had a trip off and a 'Spare Spanner' took over my ship. That's the name we give the poor blighters who mostly kick their heels ashore in idleness because there aren't enough ships to go round; and naturally these spare Skippers are very anxious to make good, by coming home with their fish-holds crammed, when they do get a chance. Only fish counts, remember.

Well, he sailed down the Humber with two other ships, and they steamed together until they reached this very spot where I'm fishing now. But luck was against him from first to last. On Christmas Eve the Spare Spanner was nearly blown off the face of the water. The other two vessels ran for shelter into a near-by fjord, and celebrated Christmas in comfort. He towed and shot and hauled outside, and faced the weather, although the other two skippers wirelessed him to come inside, warning him that the gale was likely to increase.

But he battled on, and for three weeks he fished under hellish conditions, and without hardly a blink of sleep. His total days of fishing numbered fifteen. The others came out and fished for only seven days. On the twenty-sixth day, after leaving the Humber, the Spare Spanner limped through the lock-pits with the whole of his crew and himself dead beat. The market was against him, and although he had had a record catch, his fish made only £600-a loss-and he settled in debt. The other two ships sailed in the day after, with half the amount of fish, but the market had soared. One made £1,800 and the other £1,750, over £1,000 gross profit each.

The luck of the game! Only figures count. The Spare Spanner went back to his clogs.

Remorseless! Aye, remorseless, but read these extracts from my log:

Tuesday, January 18th.-Hauled at 1 p.m. Wind increasing to gale force, E.N.E. Visibility nil.

Shipping seas. Men can't stand in the fish pounds. Only 20 baskets last haul, all sprags. Not even a living.

Working Burie Deep.

Midnight, same date. -Net fast. Second split since 6 p.m. Big tear in belly. Seas still running. Gale increasing. Conditions hellish. Caught only 100 baskets of fish in last 24 hours. The lads are dead beat.

My eyes are heavy through want of sleep. Haven't had a rodger (sleep) since Sunday morning. Now Wednesday morning. No sign of weather easing. The longer this lasts the longer we must remain out.

Provisions for only 26 days this trip. If this wind keeps up we'll soon be on salt junk and biscuit. We must remain out to cover our expenses.

Expenses to date £130, and less than 300 boxes stowed. The fish may bring 2s. 6d. per box, or they may bring 5s., but whatever they bring, at this rate of fishing, its long odds we'll settle in debt-below the thin red line.

Wednesday, January 19th.-Been dodging about all night, laying, and risking an occasional haul. Seas are like bloody mountains. She's chucking the water about. Wind veered to the Nor'ard. No sign of a living yet. Time 10 a.m.

Noon, same date.-Just hauled. Fish on the move. Cod's bellies full of sand eels. One big sprag had well over a thousand eels packed in its maw.

Six p.m., same date.-Picked up a dead cow in net last haul. Heaved it up on gilson, but as fast as we picked up rotten carcase it fell to pieces. Crew still vomiting with stench. Had to quarter it and lash on boards to heave overboard. Net badly split. Weather still holds. Shackle came adrift in bunt-end.

Fishing still slack-averaging only 20 baskets a haul. Just received a message from 'Sparks.' Markets flat-6,300 kit of fish sent to manure at Hull.

Midnight, same date.-Weather has eased a little, but fog about. About a dozen other trawlers towing around. Can't see them but can hear them blaring. Pulled up 40 baskets last haul, and dropped a dan buoy. Anxious hour now the dan down. I'm sticking to ground, but tempted to move.

Thursday, January 20th.-Time 4 a.m. Hauled another 40 baskets two hours ago. Success at last, I thought. Then the rain came down, and the fog thickened, and I've lost my dan buoy. £8 out of my pocket. I'm steaming to the Whaleback rock-about 20 miles to the Nor' ard.

Had a yarn over the 'air' with my nephew, Ted Hutchinson, on the Glen Kidston. Ted having a basinful. Trawled forty miles last two days and has hauled up only 13 baskets. Starvation! Marvellous how many miles this great, gaping net can tow the ocean deeps and bring up only a few lousy fish.

Noon, same date.-Off the Whaleback. Another bad split last haul. Rat holes in the belly fathoms long.

Might as well not been in the water . . . one hole would have let a whale through. Have laced up the bunt, and given her 25 fathoms less warp. Now we're off again, hoping to miss the 'nails.'

Received another message from Ted, my nephew. His echometer has conked out. Bad job. The lad must be nearly crazy with worry. But still he can laugh. Ted's always cheery. Heart of a lion. Have given him my position. He's steaming towards me.

3 p.m., same date.-Weather clearing a little. 22 ships towing in line. Another trawler just towed across our stern and fouled my gear. Headline broken in several places. Have laid to mend, as both trawls now split. Damn the luck

Friday, January 21st.-Time 1 p.m. Weather again decreasing to gale. Wind Northerly. Visibility nil.
Ship turning outside in. Hauled only 60 baskets all night. Still at the Whaleback. No sign of Ted.

Midnight, same date -Cast trawl at midnight. Weather growing steadily worse-wind (gale force), sleet and snow. Men have been gutting, cleaning, and mending for last 12 hours without a break-working waist deep in water-occasional sea washing them off their feet. Temperature 40 below. Will lay next haul and give them a spell.

Saturday, January 22nd.-Time, noon. Lay to all night. Strong N.E. wind. Conditions still bloody awful. Had yarn with Tom Evans on *Stoke City*. Tom reports good catches. Lucky devil. Has dropped dan buoy and given me his position.
Saturday night.-'Music Hall' and 'In Town To-night.' I always listen-in to National on Saturday nights, and enjoy a spot of music for an hour. . . . Must thank the B.B.C. one day. It brings us very near home, and it's grand to forget about fish for a short sixty minutes. We'd be very lonely without the wireless.

·　　·　　·　　·　　·　　·

But now we will close this song of woe and listen to a few moans over the 'air.' My loud speaker, behind me on the bridge, has been 'crackling' for hours, and the ether is literally blue with curses.
I can 'wig in' -overhear-any two skippers cross-talking by simply travelling up and down the wavelength of my wireless, from 100 to 160 metres on the short-wave length.
The ether vibrates with sleepy, drawly voices, and occasionally a string of staccato curses comes rippling over that makes even the hair on my experienced 'crust' rise on end.

We each keep a code book, you'll remember, and we've also got that black book handy. Our motto is 'help those that help you'-and to hell with all others. We know all the 'others.'

For hours past I've been trying to get in touch with my nephew, Ted Hutchinson, skipper of the Grimsby trawler, Glen Kidston. The lad is hard up against it, but he's a cheerful, optimistic soul, and absolutely fearless.

He calls me Pop-but here he is at last, and the young scallywag has scant respect for his uncle.

Listen in, and I'll write down the manner in which we call and receive each other over the 'air,' but I'll cut down the swear words to a minimum for the benefit of the Postmaster General.

"Glen Kidston calling the *Arsenal*... *Arsenal*-Kidston-*Arsenal*-Kidston-Glen Kidston calling the *Arsenal*-wave-length 120-120-120-Kidston-*Arsenal*-Wake up, Podgy! Hoy! Hoy! Hoy! Glen Kidston calling all trawlers Anybody seen 'Hurricane Hutch'-king of the bloody Sprags!...Kidston-*Arsenal*! .

Uncle Pop missing! I'll bet he's got ruddy great 'crust' on feathers!... Yow!... *Arsenal*!...*Arsenal*! . . .Wake up, you (censored) . . . ! Over to you, *Arsenal*! . . Are you getting me, Pop? . . . Over!"

I reply:

"Kidston-*Arsenal*-Kidston-*Arsenal*, Yow, ye young scoundrel, I can hear you a' reet, an so can all the bloody fleet. Not so much lip, young 'un, or I'll smack bottom when I lay hands on ye. How's things?. . . An' where th' hell are ye? . . . Hast tha been openin' fish shop, lad? . . . Over!"

Ted replies:

"Got you Okay, Pop, a la posh. . . . I'm off the Horns (S.E. Iceland). . Havin' a lousy packet, I can tell tha . . . fog, blizzard, and wind. . . . The damned echometer's busted, an' we haven't seen blink o' land since we left old ale town. . . No, not a sign. . . . I've got less than a hundred baskets, Pop . . . a week's bloody graft for nowt. . . . Thought the luck had turned yesterday Shot after breakfast an' got 30 baskets, 10 of ducks...shot again at noon an' hauled another 30, all sprags shot again at midnight, an' pulled full bag, but lost the bloody lot . . . the cod-end busted just as we were about to swing bag inboard . . . an' they wonder why we curse, Pop. . . . I've a good mind to go

'long ta' old pitch, Pop, you know the spot-I've had enough of this lousy ditch. . Might find a spot of fishka there what dost tha think, Pop? . . . Hast seen owt of *Leicestershire*? . . . I've been calling him for three days - has he gone home? . . . Over to you, Pop! . . . Okay pip! . . . Over!"

I reply:

"Got you, Okay, Ted. . . . Bad luck, lad, thou're havin' share o' cracks.

. . . Yow! . . . Echometer konked out? . . . That's bad. . . . But keep smiling, lad ! . . . We're havin' our share on t' *Arsenal* wrappin' nets round every damned rock on t' ditch . . . split bellies, busted wings, an' broken headlines every bloody haul . . yow! . . . But 'horsie keep yer tail up' laugh like hell, Ted . . . keep on laughin' an' curse old Feathery . . . that'll help, lad.

"No, I ain't seen owt of *Leicestershire*. . . . I'll get Sparks to gae him a bollo presently. . . No, I don't fancy th' old spot this weather. . . . I'm off to Whaleback. . . . Come along over . . . that's my advice, youngster . . . or, better still, call me again at 2 a.m. I'll have hauled next bag by then. . . . If there's any fishka about I'll gae ye th' griffen. . . . Keep smilin', lad. . . . Over !"

Ted replies:

"Hello, hello, hello ! . . . Okay, Pop, got that Okay! Two o'clock will suit me . . . I'll sit tight right here till then. . . . I hear Tom Evans on *Stoke City* calling you. Okay, Tom, I've finished with Pop. . . . Over to you, *Stoke City*. . . . Pip, pip, Pop. . . . I'm smilin'. Over !"

The *Stoke City* calls

"*Stoke City* calling *Arsenal-Arsenal*! *Arsenal*! *Arsenal*!

· . . *Stoke City* calling 'Hurricane Hutch'. . . . Pop-Eye, the sailor man. . . . Are you getting me, Pop? Over !"

I reply:

"*Arsenal* . . *Stoke City*. . . . Yow! I'm getting thou, Tom. . . . Back to you, lad. . . . Over!"

He replies:

"Hello, Albert! Thought thou'd gone touring, t'South America. . . . I've been wigging' to y' yarn wi Ted. . . . Th' lad's havin' a bellyful, isn't he? . . . An' so say all of us. . . Hauled ten lousy (censored) bags last flop . . an' a tidal wave smashed aboard an' swept ruddy lot back in t' pond. . . . Yow I . . . Nearly lost a man as well, Pop . . . th' third hand. . . . I'm prowlin' along on yer stern, Pop . . . trying to dig a few more out. . . . Now't doin' yet. . . . Heard you ask for *Leicestershire*. . . . She's just steamed for home, Pop. Lucky blighters! . . . I've stowed 10-25-20-40 baskets last four hauls, all (censored) sprags How hast thou got on, Albert? . . . Over !"

I reply:

"Aye, aye, Tom! ...got you, O.K. . . . I've beaten thee to-day, lad. . . . Hauled 150 baskets, mostly sprags an' codling, but prime fish, prime swag. . . . Aye, we're havin' rough time. . . . It wouldn't be so bad if Old Feathery would let up and gae us a bit of break.

I got fast again last haul. . . . 'Had a hellofa job getting her round to windward . . . made certain she'd sit on gear an' get propeller tied up. . . . Lay to all night repairing port net. . . . The fish are here, Tom. . . . I can smell them That's why I'm sticking. . . . This weather can't last for ever. . .

. I'll throw bit of a blister if it's worth it. . . . Just going to poke her in, an' risk another go. . . . I'll let you know how we get on. Over to you, Tom."

Tom replies

"Got that all O.K., Albert. . . We're fishing in seventy (fathoms). . . . I'll come back again about midnight. . . . Cheerio, Albert! . . .. Hope you strike a few, but if this weather doesn't let up we'll all be on ruddy dole. . . . I've gone!"

Now listen to these two skippers cross~talking

Alf Evans, skipper of the *Jean Eva*, and 'Mae' West, of the Nighi Watch. Alf is the elder brother of Tom Evans, and although he belongs to the Consolidated he refused to have his ship called after a football team. The *Jean Eva* is called after his daughter.

"Quit swearing, Alf;" shouts 'Mae' over the 'air'-(you ought to hear him curse sometimes). "quit swearing, you naughty, naughty Alf; or I'll send for my Solicitors."

Skipper West continues : "We're up wrong bloody turning this trip, Alfie . . never mind, we can have some fish an' chips when 's get back t'old Ale town. Yow!

"That's if old woman has any ruddy dough left when 's do get back. Can't expect owt fa' gaffers wi' no ruddy sprags in t' hold. My old dutch works on t' theory that tha can find what tha wants when tha don't want it by looking where it wouldn't be if tha didn't want it, but I'll bet she couldn't find any sprags in this lousy ditch, Alfie, no matter where she looked. I can't find any. How art thou gettin' on, lad?

"Just heard 'Hurricane Hutch' yarnin' wi' 's nephew just now-'Hurricane Hutch, King of the Sprags.' Hast tha heerd 'ould lad's written book, Alfie? I'll bet 'e doan't tell truth. Naw-he dursn't.

"Tha knows, Alfie, last neet ould 'Hurricane an me had bust-up ashore, he scoffed 24 dozen oysters, a ruddy great meat an' p'taita pie, an' ten ruddy sandwiches up in t' Nellie's room-yow! What a gut! An' next time. I seen 'im-th' same neet, Alfie, th' same neet-he was parked outside Royal Hotel wi' a ruddy great paper full o' fish an' chips-an' he had 's collar an' tie off-so's thrapple cud work easy like. . . . Yow!

"Why haven't you been on th' air, Alfie? I've been trying to get tha for days past. Hast tha been ashore for hike, lad? . . . Over I"

Skipper Alf Evans replies. His voice is hoarse, and guttural, and blares over the 'air' like a fog horn:

"Got ya, got ya, Mae, got ya O.K. Well, this lousy job's nuff ta mak' ye swear, lad. I've enough ruddy trouble of ma own, Mae, that's the reason a-haven't been on t' air, lad.

"Everybody moanin' an' groanin' . . It's allus ruddy same in't' slack fishin'.

"Tak' what God sends, I say. I'm close inta th' 'Papeys,' but there's nothin' but ruddy coalies here (red fish). But I'm not chuckin' overboard, lad, na, I'm not chuckin' 'em back. They're better than nowt.

"I had a basinful last haul, Mae. . . . Agin tha wind when she came fast on't 'nail' . . . hung on, split the wings, broke the headlines, tore ruddy belly out, an' swag-bag came up empty . . . not a ruddy sprag in cod-end. Three hours battlin' for nowt . . . and people wonder why we swear, Mae. . . . If ruddy P. M.G. had ta come an' get 's own fish I'll bet he'd curse sometimes. . . . Yow

"Still, there's others worse off than us, Mae. I'd go bloody daft if I'd Ted Hutchinson's trouble. Th' lad hasn't had crust on feathers for week, an' nowt ta show for 's graft. . . . An' all for tha love of a woman, Mae, all for the love of a woman. . . . God bless 'em!

"I'm closing down now, Mae. I'll gae ye shout at dawn, !ad. I'm just going ta have a yarn with my son on th' *Leicestershire* before he gets out of range. . . . I've gone !"

Seven days later my nephew, Ted, again speaks to me over the 'air.' All this time he has been towing blind, his echometer out of action, buffeted unmercifully by incessant gales and fog. There is no hope of him now making up the leeway. His coal and provisions are fast running out, and soon he must run for home . . . and sign in debt, below the fatal red line.

•   •   •   •   •   •

Back to my log book, and the date is Saturday, 29th January, 1938. Again my loud-speaker blares, and here is the entry:

"No, Pop, we haven't had a dog's chance. Nor'east, Nor'east gales, fog, and blizzard, all the time, blowin' us inside out. Splits, broken lines, an' busted bellies every haul, and the lads can hardly stand upright on their feet. What a lousy game!

"I've had enough, Pop, yow! I've had a basinful. . . Brain's very, very weary. Things are very finickitif; otherwise funookitif The old P.M.G. won't find these words in any dictionary, Pop, but they're fisherman's language . . . substituted for other words unprintable...meaning that things are bloody bad.

"But it's all in the game, Pop, all in the game, and as old Aif Evans says, I guess we've got to take what God sends us, and be thankful. Yow!

"God feeds the ravens,' Pop. I've heard you say that...wonder if gaffers'll say that to me when I get home?

"Well, okadok, Pop, okadok, and pip, pip. I'm going to have one last circular tour after 'ducks' (haddocks) before my coal runs out, and then it's me for the old Ale town.

"Au revoir, Pop ! I've gone !"

Leicestershire, one of the latest and most modern of the Grimsby fleet, owned by the *Leicestershire* Steam Fishing Company, and managed by H. Markham Cook Ltd., was homeward bound from the Icelandic grounds and was due in Grimsby last Monday, 24th January.

On Thursday night, 27th January, she was in radio communication with the Northern Chief and her position was then given as 40 miles north-west of the Skerries, then, at 1.44 a.m. on Friday, she was in touch with Wick Radio Station, when her position was given as 30 miles northwest of Sules Skerries.

That was the last heard of her.

Another entry in my log dated Monday, 31st January, 1938, reads Yesterday, Sunday, 3oth January, four bodies and a ship's boat were washed ashore at Hoy. The boat bore the name of the maker, R. Pickersgill and Co., Thornabyon-Tees, which indicated that it had come from a trawler built by Smith's Dock Co., while it also bore letters which appeared to be Grimsby.

Later a portion of a Marconi set was washed ashore, and with this, fears became certainty, for it bore a serial number which established the fact that it had come from the *Leicestershire*.

•   •   •   •   •   •

The aftermath-extract from the Grimsby Evening Telegraph, Monday, 7th February, 1938:

Six Grimsby fishermen, victims of the disaster to the Grimsby trawler *Leicestershire*, near the island of Hoy in the Orkneys, came home to Grimsby for the last time last night on board the Grimsby trawler *Hampshire*.

Their return home was made possible only through a chain of circumstances.

Skipper Albert Meach, who commands *Hampshire*, is a brother-in-law of Skipper A. D. Evans, who commanded the ill-fated *Leicestershire*.

Skipper Meach was homeward bound from the Icelandic fishing grounds when he learned through the radio of the disaster to the *Leicestershire* and that bodies had been found on the shore at Hoy. At that time it was thought possible that one of the bodies was that of Skipper Evans and Skipper Meach promptly wirelessed to his owners in Grimsby that he was calling at Longhope to see if he could assist in the sad task of identifying the victims.

It was seen that *Hampshire* could make the call and still be in time to catch the markets today and permission was wirelessed to Skipper Meach to bring back to Grimsby those bodies which were identified. Owing to the police regulations it was not possible to remove any bodies which remained unidentified, and desperate efforts were made at Grimsby to complete as many identifications as possible in the short space of time available.

It was then found that the body which had been thought to be that of Skipper Evans was another member of the crew of the lost trawler.

Just before *Hampshire* arrived at Longhope, however, another body was seen from the shore and the islanders finally succeeded in recovering it. Skipper Meach promptly identified the body as that of his brother-in-law, but despite every effort it was found impossible to identify two of the men and they had to be buried at Longhope.

Skipper Meach readily agreed to bring the other six men home to Grimsby, but a further difficulty arose as, owing to the sparsely-populated nature of the islands, it was not possible to obtain sufficient coffins in the Orkneys. This difficulty was speedily overcome by *Hampshire* making a special journey to Stromness and returning to Longhope with two more coffins.

By this means *Hampshire* was able to leave Longhope on Saturday with six coffins on board, arriving in the River Humber late yesterday afternoon.

Special arrangements were made so that *Hampshire* should be the first vessel to enter the docks as soon as the lock gates were opened, and about 7.30 p.m. her deck lights were seen gleaming across the still water as she steamed slowly through the lock gates and across the dock to the berth which had been reserved for her.

By this time there was a small crowd of about a couple of hundred men lining the quayside and as *Hampshire* approached every head was bared. Prominent in the crowd was a silent little group of six men, Skipper Alfred Evans, of the Grimsby trawler, *Jean Eva*, father of the dead skipper, and five other men, all relatives of the dead skipper. Here and there in the crowd stood other men whose black ties proclaimed that they, too, had come to see their lost relatives make their last landfall on this earth.

On board *Hampshire*, her crew, bareheaded, lined the rail, not a sound breaking the silence as *Hampshire* came in to the quayside.

Even the task of bringing the ship alongside and mooring her was accomplished in a, strange silence.

When the ship was safely moored the first person to board her was Mr. H. Markham Cook, managing owner of both *Leicestershire* and *Hampshire*.

He was closely followed by his ship's husband, Mr. Pegg, and by Mr. J. V. Chatburn, assistant secretary of the Grimsby Steam Fishing Vessels Mutual Insurance and Protection Co., Ltd., and Skipper Evans, senior. The few brief formalities necessary were soon completed and the task of removing the coffins was commenced.

Motor hearses had been waiting at the edge of the fish market in readiness.

The six coffins, all of them plain black with black fittings, as is the custom in the Orkneys, were reverently removed from their resting-place underneath the whale back of the *Hampshire* and laid out upon the deck.

Members of the crew of *Hampshire* moved forward to act as bearers and perform their last service for their comrades, but they were checked by Skipper Evans.

"You have done enough," he said. "This is our job now." He and his five relatives insisted upon acting as bearers for all the coffins. The first one to be lifted ashore was that of Skipper Evans, Jun., it being handled solely by his relations.

The crowd parted and lined the few yards' width of the fish market to where the hearses were in waiting. A minute or two later the coffin containing the body of Harold Burkitt was lifted on to the quayside where, under the glare of the electric floodlights on the quayside, it was borne to another hearse.

The remaining four coffins, which contained the remains of Hubert Lamisher Lancaster, a fireman; Alfred William Booth, the third hand ; Harold James Symonds, a fireman; and Christopher Slater, the chief engineer, were, in turn, reverently carried ashore to the waiting hearses.

Immediately afterwards Skipper Evans returned on board *Hampshire*, where he shook hands with every member of the crew and thanked them for all they had done.

A few minutes later the crew of Hampshire climbed over the side of their ship with the kit bags on their shoulders the crowd dispersed, and in a few minutes the quayside was deserted.

Meantime a crowd of several hundred people had gathered at the level crossing gates at Fish Dock Road and in Riby Square. Entrance to the Fish Docks had been restricted by the L.N.E. Railway Police to the relatives and those who had legitimate business on the docks so as to spare the relatives as much as possible. Consequently, the crowd of spectators had to remain outside the dock gates, but as the hearses left the docks every man there bared his head.

At the dock gates were a few tragic women dressed in black. They had lost relatives in the disaster, and their bodies had not been recovered. They eagerly questioned those who had witnessed the landing of the coffins, hoping against hope that their menfolk might have been found and brought home to them, but their vigil was in vain.

The coffins were removed to the Fishermen's Church, the Tiverton Street Bethel Mission, where they were received by the Port Missioner, Mr. Harold Pickering. There the coffins will remain until the joint funeral service on Tuesday afternoon at 2 p.m.

Tomorrow the relatives will be admitted to the church from 4 p.m. until 5 p.m. to pay their private homage. After 5 p.m. the general public will be enabled to pay their last respects to the six sailors who have come home from the sea for the last time.

Last evening a magnificent wreath in the form of an anchor in red and white chrysanthemums was received at the Bethel Mission. It bore the inscription "To the memory of fifteen brave sailors" and was from the directors and staff of Messrs. H. Markham Cook, Ltd.

The price of fish!

Chapter 8

OVERLAND BILLY

Aboard S.T. Arsenal.
Trawling Lat. 63° 24" N. Long 41° 26" W

We've steamed a little to the Nor'ard since my last entry in this log, and I'm now in what we call the 'Bumping Ground,' off the Papyes.

The Papyes are two great mountains off this Iceland coast shaped very much like a woman's breasts.

Overnight the weather has changed to half a gale, and we're shipping it green.

Since 1 a.m. this morning-it's now 8 a.m.-we've been dodging about, laying to, riding it out, and risking an occasional haul. That's not easy when the ruddy seas are sweeping us from stem to stern, and the decks are like a half-tide rock.

I nearly lost Alex Baines, last haul; Abe, my mate, grabbed him by the ankles just as he was going overboard.

A near thing!

We've only pulled up twenty baskets all night-eight stone of fish to the basket. We must average fifty baskets a haul to make a living. When I do strike the tail-waggers (if I do), I shall have to drive the brats like hell to make up the leeway.

Yesterday there were nearly a hundred ships around here, Yorkies (Hull), Grimmies (Grimsby), Swannies (Swansea), and Square Heads (Germans), mostly; now I can only see three.

The *Stoke City*'s still here, and the *Jean Eva*.

Some men won't work this ground because the bottom's littered with rocks and wreckage. That means plenty of splits (torn nets). That's why we call it the bumping ground. But I don't care a damn how many splits I get as long as my cod-end comes up bursting with sprags.

Splits can be mended.

So some of us stick it, and blast old Feathery Legs. That's the only secret in this game, as I've said before-you've got to stick till the last gasp, no matter how bad the luck or weather. Get the wind up in this gamble, start smoke-chasing, as we call it - steaming around wasting coal and wasting valuable time-and sure as blazes ye'll miss the fish.

Sit tight and keep crackin' Keep that trawl on the bottom! That's my advice to all young skippers and mates.

Patience! Curse old Feathery, curse the ship, curse the crew, curse the P.M.G., keep on cursing.

That'll help you to stick. Yow!

When I was skipper of the *Green Howard* some years ago, I came here regularly every trip for months, a lone ship. No one else would work this lousy ground. Splits! Hell! It was torn wings, split bellies, and broken headlines every haul.

I worked the brats till they fell asleep in the fish pounds, but I caught fish, aye, an' plenty, even if I had to have a fresh crew every trip. 'Hurricane Hutch'! Well, I don't care a damn what they call me.

I've been through the mill myself, and even although I'm now Johnny-the-One, for every hour the brats spend in the pounds I'm prepared to spend two on the bridge. Yow!

The bogey-man's still in the offing (the Iceland gunboat), blast him! We greet him occasionally through the megaphone as we sweep past, and give him a few blurts. Like the P.M.G.-the bloke who fines trawlermen for swearing over the mike-he knows every syllable of our language backwards.

Reckon Mr. Bogey-man 'ud rather face a gun than the megaphone of either a Yorkie or a Grimmie.

I've got Alex Baines, my leading deckhand, beside me on the bridge just now, and we've just had a yarn about one or two scraps we've had wi' bogeyman. As I told you before, this ewe lamb has the strength of three normal men, and the shoulders of a bullock. His great paws, always black with tar from the nets-an' you can't tell nail from flesh-are cracked and cut with a hundred scars. He never shaves at sea, none of us do, and to see him now, his black whiskers sprouting out like porcupine quills, you might easily mistake him for an enormous ape. But he's the finest deckie sailing the Northern Seas, and he's almost human.

Alex eats his fish, about ten big haddocks at a sitting, with a fork, and removes the bones. The rest of the brats eat them with their fingers-unfilleted, bones an' all.

Alex nods towards the distant gunboat "D'you remember that afternoon when that blighter nearly got us, Skipper?"

Hell! Do I remember it? "Yes, almost in this very spot where we're fishing now, Alex."

Alex nodded grimly. "Yow! Reckon the fog saved our bacon that afternoon."

We lapsed into silence for a moment.

"I reckon the skipper of the gunboat got our number that day," said Alex absently. "If he hadn't died, I guess we'd have been for the high jump afterwards."

"You've said a mouthful," I agreed laconically "Luck was certainly with us," I added.

Aye, bogey-man nearly got me that afternoon.

We were fishing just outside the limit-line, hugging the coast, and fishing had been slack for days. I knew that just inside the line the tail-waggers were there in shoals, and it's a sore temptation to keep to the law when your bread and butter, as it were, is lying there almost under your nose. Then the fog came down, almost without warning, as it has a habit of doing along this coast, and I drifted inside the fatal line-by accident.

"We didn't know we were inside the line-did we, Alex?"

Alex grinned and winked slyly.

"Of course we didn't, Skipper!" He cackled loudly, like a hen laying an egg.

At any rate, we made one haul under cover of the fog and yanked out ninety baskets of flats-900 stone of prime flat fish, young halibut, plaice, and soles.

Still the fog held, and although it was bright daylight high overhead, we could hardly see the whaleback from the bridge. The fo'c'sle peak of a trawler is called a whaleback because its design is very much like the back of a whale.

"It's a wonder we didn't run the blighter down," again chuckled Alex.

"By heck, you're right, Alex!"

We shot the trawl a second time, and, just as we steamed ahead, bogey-man loomed up in the mist and we towed slap alongside the grey hulk of the gunboat. In fact, we didn't see the ugly blighter until the commander hailed us from the bridge.

"Heave to!" he blared, through a megaphone, in English. "Heave to, or I fire!"

It was a fair cop. There didn't seem a dog's chance of getting away, and to make certain of a capture he barged alongside, hugging my rails.

"Run aft, Alex," I whispered quickly-he was beside me on the bridge. "Jump to it!" I ordered tersely, "and get the chopper ready," I added hoarsely.

Alex understood, and scrambled down the bridge ladder with the agility of a monkey, and Alex can streak like greased lightning when needs be.

"Heave to!" yelled the commander again.

"O.K.!" I howled back. "But give me room to haul in my gear," I added. "Lay off a bit!"

He backed off; and as soon as he cleared my rails I barked an order down the speaking tube to the engine-room.

"Give her all she's got, Chief," I snapped, at the same time I tugged fiercely on the siren lanyard above my head.

That whistle gave Alex his cue. With two quick swipes of his axe he chopped the trawl warps, and, once free of the great net dragging astern, the ship shot ahead at speed.

Slap into the mist, thick as pea-soup, we barged hell for leather, setting a course out to sea. We heard him yelling behind us, and then the loud roar of a gun.

I ducked, but nothing happened, no noise of screaming shell.

A blank!

There were plenty of other trawlers about-dozens of them. We could hear their fog-signals blaring all around us-to starboard, to port, and dead ahead. But we steamed full pelt into the driving mist, and trusted to Providence we wouldn't hit some unlucky pal in the guts.

Bang! Another blank. Bang! Three blanks!

I could see the grey outline of his stem churning the waters just behind us.

"Open her up, Chief, open her up," I spat down the speaking tube. "He'll barge into our stern in a minute."

"She's all out, Skipper," the Chief hissed back. "The bloody boilers'll bust if I give her any more."

I opened the bridge window. The brats were all leaning over the rails for'ard, their eyes glued on the chasing gunboat.

"Get down into the stoke-hold - all of you," I yelled. Then I dashed back into the wheelhouse.

"Chief, I'm sending the brats down to give you a hand. Stoke her up," I ordered tersely, "and let her bust."

On we steamed for another few minutes, and I had one eye glued ahead, although we could barely see a yard, and my head half-turned with the other eye glued on the grey stem behind.

Gradually we drew ahead.

"Go on, Chief," I again hissed down the tube. "Let her have it, we're showing him our heels."

Bang! A shell whined over the wheel-house. A live one this time, and how. It screamed past the wheelhouse roof, missing it only by inches.

I ducked again, and lay flat on the floor.

Bang! Bang! Bang! Over they came, and I was now flat on my back, one hand steering the wheel, the other clawing on to the whistle lanyard, blowing like hell, and both eyes glued on the swinging compass overhead. If we hit anything at this speed-heaven help us both.

Still we barged ahead, and still the shells came screaming out of the mist, the gunboat firing blind.

He pumped eight live shells in our direction, and chased us for forty miles, but never caught up.

All that time I lay on my back steering the ship, and praying for a spot of luck.

We had more than luck that day. Providence was on our side.

The gunfire ceased at last, and we eased down and listened.

Not a sound! Far away, beyond the thick curtain of swirling fog, we heard the distant echoes of sirens, but they were faint, and we were all alone.

Then we hove to, put out a new trawl, and commenced fishing again.

"D'you think he got our number, Skipper?" My mate asked the question later. Our numbers, and the letters of our home port, are painted in big white letters as large as an average man's height, on both
sides of the vessel.

"He must have done," I said grimly.

"Then it's you for the high jump, Skipper," said the mate. "Better make tracks for home. He'll scour the seas for us as soon as this fog lifts."

"I'll take a chance," I said. My fish-holds were less than half full.

So we fished on, and next morning a message reached us over the air.

The gunboat had captured another trawler within the limit-line shortly after he abandoned the chase after us.

It was then that Providence took a hand in the game. That morning, as he was giving evidence in court ashore, against the Skipper of the captured trawler - a mate of mine, incidentally - the gunboat commander suddenly collapsed in the witness-box and died of heart failure.

Thus, our own case was never recorded.

"Yes, I guess if he hadn't died as he did," said Alex absently, "we'd have been for the high jump, all right."

I agreed.

Alex deftly rolled a cigarette, running a fat, bright-red tongue reflectively down the gummed edge.

"D'you remember Overland Billy, Skipper?" asked Alex.

I laughed.

"What, old Bill Loftus ! Will anyone ever forget that hair-brained blighter? By hell, he was the boy for bogey-man."

Alex lit his cigarette, pursing his lips in a queer, twisted grin.

"And don't I know it," he growled. "That basket"-Alex didn't say basket, but a word very like it-"nearly got me hung umpteen times. I sailed with him for three bloody years. Aye, and they were bloody. We were captured twice within a few months, not counting the number of scraps we had in between, and, as you know, Billy finally got ten years for laying out the captain of the gunboat *Philla*."

I gave the wheel a twist and prepared to listen. Old Charlie, the cook, waltzed into the wheelhouse with three steaming mugs of tea. We drink about ten quarts each a day at sea, all hands. That's practically our sole beverage when we're fishing-trawlermen's beer. There's always a big urn of tea standing on the galley stove, night and day, and I reckon a tax on tea hits us more than any section of the community ashore, not excluding the old grannies, male or female.

"Sit down, Charlie." I pointed to one of the high desk stools in the wheelhouse. "Alex's going to give us a crack about some of his adventures with Overland Billy-you remember Billy Loftus, don't you?"

"That basket!" Charlie passed round the tea. "Go on, Alex, get crackin'. I know the whole story backward, but I can listen again. If the grub's spoilt, don't blame me."

"What's for dinner to-day, Cookie?" asked Alex, wiping his grimy lips.

"Thinking of your guts already," growled Charlie. "Hell, you've only just had your breakfast. . . twelve haddocks he scoffed, Skipper," said Charlie, addressing me, "twelve bloody haddocks, six rashers of bacon a bloody great helpin' o' hash left over from last night and finished up with a whole cob of bread and about half a pound of strawberry jam."

"Yes, an' I've got to pay for it, me and the mate," I said, "not the bloody gaffers."

Alex grinned. "That's your fault," he chortled "If you stand for the share system, and gamble the catch for your wages, then you've got to foot the bill. You can't expect the gaffer's to pay for the grub and the coal, and give you fellows a bloody great whack out of the profits as well."

"Profits!" I spluttered savagely. "An' last voyage my fish brought less than a penny a pound on the market, and half the catch sent to the manure dump. What d'you call that, Alex? You fellows are a damned sight better off than us. At least your wages are certain. You can always be sure of taking something home to the wife and kids after each voyage, but we skippers and mates can't say same."

"And whose fault is that?" Charlie chipped "Not the gaffers. The lousy, pot-bellied buyers get all the cream out of this game, aye, and the milk well, blast them !"

Alex tugged open the wheelhouse window, and expectorated with precision. The spit might land on the head of a deckie on the for'ard deck below but these things did not concern Alex.

"Yes, I'd like to have a few of these blood suckers in the fish-pounds, just to show them what this lousy game is like sometimes. I bet one dose'd be enough for them. They grab our fish at less than a penny a pound nearly all the year round, but my missus is never able to buy even the cheapest variety under sixpence a pound . . . and that goes for all the public."

"Aye," said Charlie. "An' our wives are living in hovels down Grimsby way, whilst their wives are living on the hill, in mansions, wi' big gardens, an' cars . . . you never see a deckie wi' a bloody car."

Alex drank a pint of tea at a gulp.

"Aw, to hell wi' them," he grunted disgustedly. "You haven't told me what's for dinner yet."

Cook appealed to me for sympathy.

"Listen to him, Skipper," he gasped. "Here we're discussin' a subject that affects the-the whole British Commonwealth, an' all he thinks about is grub."

"Then for heaven's sake tell him, Charlie," I say. "He'll keep on until you do."

Charlie enumerated on his fingers. "Well, there's soup, roast beef, carrots, peas, mashed potatoes, rice pudding, fruit, tea, and pancakes-and if that's not enough for your big, fat gut," he added in disgust, "there's a dish of cold fish left over from breakfast."

Alex snorted. "Is that all," he growled. "When dl' hell are you gonna give us some grub to eat?"

Charlie spluttered.

"D'you hear him, Skipper? D'you hear him? I'll bet his missus doesn't give him as much in a week as we give him at one meal."

"The poor lass can't afford to," snarled Alex bitterly. "The lousy buyers an' middlemen see to that."

He glanced at the bridge clock. "When are you hauling, Skipper?" he asked, changing the subject.

"In twenty minutes, and if you two don't drop this argument I'm turning in for a rodger."

"Let him tell us about Overland Billy first," said Cook.

"O.K., but get crackin' this time, Alex; no more bloody arguments."

Alex carefully rolled another cigarette.

"Well," he began, "you know why we call him Overland Billy? To save coal and time Loftus preferred to hit rocks than go round. He knocked more pieces off the Iceland coast any other skipper who ever sailed out of Grimsby.

"Bill was a small, lean fellow, about thirty when I sailed with him, and as quick and wiry as a monkey. Scrap! Hell, he'd take on two men, big as houses, an' lick the steam out of the best. He'd no fear, neither of man nor devil, and he was always laughing. I can't remember Bill Loftus without a grin on his face.

"Sometimes he carried his wife aboard with and she was just the opposite type-a quiet, homely little buddy that'd never say boo to a dead sprag. And he used to poach with her aboard, as although she tried to prevent him.

"One day-we were on the trawler *Olaf* at the time-three of us crept into *Arma Fjord*, off the Norwegian coast, and commenced to poach inside the limit-line. The *Saint Cyia*, a Yorkie, was just in front of us, and the third trawler, towing almost abeam, was called the *Newfoundland*, a big German ship, and the skipper could speak English perfectly.

"Before we'd been in an hour a gunboat suddenly swept out of a creek and pounced on the *Saint Cyia*. Billy chopped his gear and got away slick, the big Jerry steaming behind.

"Shortly afterwards we saw the bogey-man appear back up the creek hugging the stern of the captured trawler."

Alex laughed grimly.

"Do you know what the daft blighter did as soon as the gunboat disappeared, Skipper?" he asked.

I shook my head.

"Damn me, if Billy didn't about ship and steam back again up the fjord...back on to the very same pitch," said Alex.

"Some nerve!" I breathed.

"Nerve!" He did more than that. Night was coming on, and he dropped a dan so's he could see to fish the pitch in the darkness."

"And so's the gunboat could see the light if he came snooping round again?"

"Exactly! But Bill's argument against that was sound. His wife became hysterical, and pleaded with him to clear out.

"Said Bill 'Clear out ! Not bloody likely. Yon gunboat has to escort the other trawler to the nearest port. It'll take him at least twelve hours to get back here.

"Steaming back up the fjord we met the big German coming down, and he hove alongside.

'Where the hell are you going, Bill?' Jerry yelled through his megaphone.

'I'm going back,' sang out Billy cheerfully.

My daughter Charlottes wedding to Arthur Jones

The end of the *Arsenal*

Fishermen at war

Dorothy (my best friend) and Albert

Bridge party of the newly launched *Sheffield Wednesday*

Dorothy and Albert with family

Aye, aye Skipper

Homeward Bound

'You've got a bloody cheek. Dropping a dan buoy, as well. I'm clearing t'hell out of it. That ugly basket'll be back here presently,' howled the German.

"The big German trawler cleared out, but Bill fished the fjord all night, and scooped up about 300 baskets of lovely flats."

Alex rolled his eyes.

"My word, yon were lovely fish, Skipper," he said, almost in reverence. "Clean and as firm as a virgin's bubs...

"We fished on till daylight, and at the first streak of dawn there was Bill perched straddle-legged on the roof of the swaying wheel-house, with his glasses glued to his eyes, whilst on the bridge below the frantic wife howled for him to come down and clear out.

"We crept out of the fjord shortly after breakfast, and damn me we'd just got outside the limit-line when the long, grey gunboat appeared.

"Bill gave him a long blurt on the siren and cleared off at speed."

Alex paused to light his cigarette.

"Did he chase you?" asked Charlie.

"No. Bill had painted out his number before he went into the fjord overnight, and at dawn that morning, or rather after we packed up, we painted in the original number again.

"A few weeks later," continued Alex, "we were poaching in one of the Iceland fjords one night, and shortly after dawn a gunboat pounced down on us, and ordered Bill to pull his trawl in. Billy told him to go to hell, and fished on.

"The gunboat then dropped a small motor-boat, manned by an officer and two men, but Bill ordered all hands to the rails, and told us not to let them board.

"We all had short hawks, iron battens, boat-hooks, and Bill dashed into the galley and came out armed with a murderous great poker. The cook had a bucket of hot water, with a rope attached to the handle.

'If you baskets try to come aboard my ship,' yelled Bill, 'I'll knock yer bloody brains out.'

"As soon as the motor-boat hove alongside, the cook chucked the bucket of scalding water at them, bucket an' all. It hit one of the 'scrubs,' split his head open, and laid him unconscious.

"'One out!' howled Bill. 'Come on, you baskets!'

"Both the other men in the small boat made a spring for the rails. Bill cracked the officer over the head with the poker-a wild, vicious swipe-and he dropped back into the boat, out for a week.

Somebody clamped the other fellow's fingers with a short hawk as he grabbed the rail, and he went out for the count.

"Billy next chopped his gear, and steamed like blazes for the open sea, and as the gunboat had to wait to pick up the bodies, we got clear away.

"That very same night we crept into another fjord farther up the coast, and commenced poaching again. In the small hours of the morning, whilst it was still dark, we saw the lights of another gun-boat approach. He steamed round us, shone his spotlight on the funnel, and took our number, but he didn't attempt to board us.

"Immediately he cleared out, Billy hauled the trawl, and steamed back to the place, cool as you like, where we'd had the scrap that morning.

"Daring! I'll say it was, but then, that was like Bill; he didn't care a damn for nowt.

"We towed until daylight, came fast, and got a split, so we heaved up and steamed for Stalberg corner.

"When we got there, about noon, we found about twenty other trawlers working the ground and the big Iceland gunboat steaming in between them, examining their numbers. It wasn't the same bogey-man that we'd had the scrap with, but we were quite certain that he was looking for us.

"Bill was down below having his dinner at the time, but the mate sent down a message to the cabin and told him that his presence was urgently required on the bridge.

"As soon as he came up Bill eased the ship down to slow, so as the gunboat might think we were towing instead of steaming. He also altered course gradually edged away from the fleet, and as soon as we topped tile horizon he rang her to full ahead again, and cleared like hell back on a southerly course.

"We made for the Vestman Isles, had four more hauls there, all inside the limit-line, and landed 220 baskets of lemons.

"Several people ashore observed us, and we learnt afterwards-very soon afterwards-that they sent a wireless message to the big gunboat, giving our position.

"We hadn't a wireless ourselves, but an Iceland trawler, fishing not far from us, picked up the message, and as he was a pal of Billy's, he at once came and tipped us off.

'Get to hell out of it, Bill,' he yelled through the megaphone, 'the bogey-man's coming after you pronto-clear off home.'

"But daredevil Bill risked another haul, and waited until he actually saw the gunboat sheer over the horizon before he hauled in, and cleared for Grimsby.

"Our loot consisted of 360 boxes of plaice, 220 boxes of lemon soles, 200 boxes of ducks (haddocks), 600 boxes
of sprags (cods), 600 score of big cats (cat fish), and we made £1,250, nearly all scooped up inside the limit-line.

"On our next trip we went to the White Sea, and at once commenced poaching. Billy's luck held good -and he was a lucky devil-until the very last haul of the trip, nay, the last twenty minutes of the trip. "We fished on for nearly three weeks, poaching the whole of the time, and never a sign of bogey-man.

"Then, one night, hugging the loom of the land, with all our lights dowsed, our fish-holds crammed, and waiting to haul for the last time, a searchlight suddenly stabbed the darkness dead ahead.

"We chopped the gear, and prepared to run, but he fired three blank shells at point-blank range, still sweeping us with his spot-light. He was right on top of us, and as we knew that his fourth round would be a live shell, which could not fail to hit us, Billy cursed, but stopped the ship.

"I was on the bridge when a Norwegian officer clambered up into the wheel-house.

"'What the hell d'you want?' Bill snarled. 'What d'you mean by firing your damned pop-gun at a peaceful British trawler, 'eh?'

'Consider yourself under arrest,' snapped the officer tersely. 'You're inside the territorial waters of Norway.'

"Bill spat, and advanced on him with clenched fists, his eyes blazing, but I hung on to his arm and he cooled off after a bit, and laughed. Hell, how he roared, and how like Bill.

"We were taken to Vardo, in Norway, under the escort of the gunboat, and a few days later Bill was hauled before the local court, lost all his fish, and was fined £350, but they didn't take away his gear.

"Nine days passed. We had a good time ashore, but Billy lay in a cell, kicking his heels in impatience, and waiting for the gaffers, back in Grimsby, to forward the money to bail him out of the local jug.

"He had a brother aboard, a deckie. Both were alike as two peas; and the police had never seen them together. That gave Bill an idea.

"He persuaded the Chief of Police to let him out on bail, promising to stay at a local hotel and to report daily until the money arrived. As the Chief was fairly certain that the fine would eventually be paid, he agreed to Bill's proposal.

"A few days later the persuasive tongue of Bill wheedled permission from the Chief of Police, a kind hearted bloke, to allow his mate to take the ship out for a few night's fishing, and as Bill had lost all his fish, the boob again agreed to this request.

"What did the bold Billy do, think you?

"He smuggled his brother into the hotel, told him to sham illness, and report every day to the police by phone, in case they twigged the difference, and the same day he sailed gaily out of the harbour on the bridge of the captured ship. Not only so, but that very night he swept that coast line inside the limit and dug up several hundred baskets of flats.

"Three days later he steamed back with his fish-hold full, and as the fine had been paid, Bill picked up brother Budge, blew the Chief a kiss from the quayside, and cleared for home.

"Before we got far on our way another trawler gave us the griffin that the cat-two cats-had been let out of the bag.

"Bill had been seen poaching near Vardo. Also, his brother had signed the release document, and as Bill had signed several other papers before this, the authorities at once saw the difference between the two signatures, and detected the fraud.

"However, we got clear away, but when Bill got back to Grimsby he discovered that his gaffers had had the wire from the Norwegian police, and Billy very promptly got the sack.

"But men of the Billy Loftus breed don't wear the clogs for long. Not long afterwards he signed as mate, on the *Bentor*, and I signed with him.

"As soon as we cleared the lockpits Billy mounted the bridge-as skipper.

"We trawled for ten days off the west coast of Iceland, and as fishing was good, Billy, for once in his hectic career, kept outside the limit-line.

"One night we were caught in a northerly gale and we ran to the south'ard for shelter. But Billy had left it late, as usual, and, in a blinding blizzard, we hit the shore at a place called Utskalar.

"For ten hours we bumped against the rocks losing our propeller, and sending up flares. It took us three hours of terrific battling to get the small boat out, but once aboard the wind sheered us on to the rocks, tearing the bottom out of her, and we were all battling for our lives in the ice-cold water, when we were rescued by a small Iceland fishing smack.

"I reckon, off and on, we've had a few wars wi' the Scrubs up north, but when old Feathery Legs grabs us we're all one big brotherhood then. These Icelanders had only scant rations aboard, but they gave us all their grub, lashed us up with hot coffee, peeled off part of their own clothing, and it was bitterly cold, and gave us their bunks as well.

"Next morning at dawn the Iceland salvage boat hove down on us, and we went back with them, and managed to tow the *Bentor* off the rocks. We were aboard that lousy ship-the salvage tug-for fifteen hours, but these blighters didn't give us either bite or sup.

"It was pitch dark when the *Bentor* was at last towed into Reykjavik harbour, and next morning at daylight, when I looked at the ship lying next to us, I nearly had a fit.

"Bill was still in bed, but I dived down into his cabin below the bridge and pulled him out by the ears.

"'Bill,' I said, 'd'you remember that gunboat we had a scrap with, some time ago?'

"'D'you mean the one that tried to board us wi' small boat ?' he growled.

" 'Aye, yon's the one, Bill,' I said.

"'What about it?' he growled again.

"'Oh, not much,' I said, 'only we're moored slap alongside her, that's all,' I added.

"Bill blinked at me for a moment, and then mounted the ladder to have a look.

"'Aye, yon's him, right enough,' he muttered, as soon as he saw the gunboat.

"He glowered in silence for a moment, and then he said, 'No sign of anybody aboard, Alex, let's give her the once-over. We might come up against her again, Alex,' he added.

"So the bold Billy walked aboard his old enemy, just to see if she was good enough to beat him for speed if ever he ran foul of her again.

"The first thing he saw, mounted for'ard, was a three-pounder gun. This had only recently been added, the authorities probably deciding that it might possibly be required after the ship's experience against Billy. He was still aboard the gunboat when the young officer he had cracked over the pan with the poker suddenly appeared in sight. Bill saw him from the distance, and scrambled aboard his own ship, and shot down into his cabin.

" 'Alex,' he yelled to me, 'd'you think that blighter saw me? You'd better lie doggo as well,' Bill added, 'or he might recognize you. We were on another ship, remember, the *Bentor*, and we prayed to heaven that we hadn't been recognized, and also prayed that the gunboat would clear out that day.

We had to stay put as our own propeller had been smashed on the rocks.

"After breakfast four of us, Billy, two deckies, and me, sat down to a nice game of solo in Billy's cabin. Before we'd dealt the second hand, two great uniformed police, armed to the teeth, barged into the cabin, followed by the young officer of the gunboat.

" 'That's your man !' said the latter, pointing to Billy, and poor old Bill was once again lugged off to the local jug.

"He lay in prison for a week waiting trial, and in the meantime we had a new propeller fixed on the *Bentor*. Then Billy was yanked before the court and fined £600, or, by default, ten years' imprisonment.

"We hung on for another week, waiting for the money to come from home, but at last we were obliged to sail without him.

"I am not certain how long he served in prison, but as everybody on the Humber was rather fond of Billy, a subscription was later raised to meet the fine, and the great Billy Loftus was freed again.

"Poor Billy! The most fearless, the most daring Skipper ever to sail the Northern Seas, he faced death a thousand times every year of his life, and yet at the end he died by a simple accident, ashore.

"He went to visit his mother one night, but finding her absent from home, and the front door locked, he walked round to the back door to gain entry that way, as he had often done before. But he found the yard door locked also, and in clambering over he fell, and the next morning he was found in a crumpled heap, with his skull fractured-dead."

Editor's Note

About two years ago, a striking indictment of the Icelandic policy directed against the British fisheries in Icelandic waters, chiefly concerning the bitter controversy of the 'limit-line,' was laid by Mr. J. Smith, the Secretary of the Grimsby Steam Fishing Vessels' Mutual Insurance and Protecting Co., Ltd., and Secretary of the Amalgamated Committee of Fishing Vessels Insurance for Grimsby, Fleetwood, Aberdeen, Shields, Lowestoft and Swansea.

The indictment, published fully in the Grimsby News, Friday, 26th June, 1936, caused a sensation throughout the fishing industry, and as very little has been done to adjust the conditions stressed, and as this subject is still the bone of intense controversy, we have thought fit to give it a permanent record in Skipper Hutchinson's memoirs.

Outrageously heavy penalties for alleged illegal fishing, and for minor technical offences, the persecution of British agents in Iceland, the attempt to enclose vast areas of water within territorial limits, and the threat to use live shells to stop trawlers are quoted by Mr. Smith as part of the policy to enrich Iceland at the expense of British fishermen.

Shortly before this indictment was published, a firm of British agents, controlled by a well-known family named Zoegas, in Reykjavik, Iceland, were hauled before the Icelandic court and accused of forwarding information to British trawlers as to the movement of the protecting gunboats. This was the last straw on the camel's back, as it were, and aroused a storm of indignation throughout the whole of the industry, amply reflected in the following chapter.

Chapter 9

THE LIMIT-LINE

Aboard S.T. Arsenal.
Trawling Lat. 63° 22" N. Long 41° 15" W.

I n the days of the Alward Brothers, Grimsby fishermen discovered the fishing-grounds off Iceland, and despite the long voyage, the uncharted and unlighted coasts, the magnetic storms, the fury of the Atlantic gales, and other dangers, they persevered until to-day the Icelandic are probably the most important of all our fishing-grounds.

Incidentally, the visits of the trawlers helped the Icelanders to some little extent; they certainly led to the better charting and the lighting of the coasts, and to better communication with the rest of Europe.

Now Iceland, freed from Denmark, and herself a national, is said to be endeavouring to secure the fishing-grounds for herself, and to oust foreign vessels, more particularly the British ones.

It is pointed out that for many years the patrol boats have hunted down foreign vessels, arresting some just outside the three-mile limit, that the fines have been extortionate, and the gear and catch were confiscated. In the few cases where an appeal has been successful, the value of the catch-sometimes running to hundreds of pounds-has not been returned. One serious pinprick is that these confiscated catches may have been sent out by the Icelanders to compete with our own fish in our own markets.

That there has been poaching is not denied, but this poaching, it is alleged, is the outcome of the Icelanders' own flagrant derelictions, for it is alleged to be well known throughout Iceland that the Icelandic fishing-boats fish inside the territorial limits, and sixteen times within four years a member of their own Parliament (the Althing) brought in a Bill to deal with this. We quote the preamble to this Bill in which it is clearly stated that all Icelanders were cognisant of this practice.

For years British and other trawlers were surprised that the

Icelanders could secure greater catches, and of better quality fish, than they could themselves. Believing that this might be due to the skill of Icelandic Skippers, or to their better knowledge of the waters, British trawler owners engaged Icelandic Skippers, but without bettering their results. Then some of our Skippers followed the Icelandic boats and discovered that their catches were secured inside the limits. Furthermore, they discovered that the Icelandic fishermen used the wireless to discover where the patrol boat was, that they were advised from agents ashore by code messages.

The Icelandic authorities also discovered this, and there followed a raid, which made a great stir at the time; but it was only the agents of British and other foreign firms that were raided and prosecuted.

Following this, the authorities set up an official bureau of agencies and endeavoured to force all foreign business into this bureau, but were not successful.

Next the Icelandic Government endeavoured to copy Norway, and already a suggestion has been thrown out that all foreign fishing vessels should be excluded from Faxa Bay.

Yet a further effort is a threat that live shells will be fired at trawlers that do not immediately stop when hailed.

These are the main facts, and a large volume of evidence has been collected in proof of them. Mr. Smith has set forth the position as follows:

MR. SMITH'S STATEMENT OF THE POSITION
(Extract from the "Grimsby News," 26th June, 1936)

"Iceland, although a small country, has during the last few years, and especially of late, loomed largely in the Press in reference chiefly to matters concerning the fishing industry. The same has been given a brief acknowledgment, both by our Government and Press, and then allowed to fade away, as though little importance attached to the items involved, which was further accentuated by the general apathy of the fishing trade itself.

"The matters at issue were mostly in reference to arrests within limits, faulty stowing of gear when lying for shelter or proceeding through the limits, use of private codes and information relative to location of patrol boats, and finally the notification that live shot would be used where necessary in future to bring up delinquent trawlers which failed to stop when ordered by patrol

"Superficially, these were in no wise apprehensive, being but the ordinary rights held by other nations, and if applied equitably, demanded little criticism.

"But to those persons behind the scenes and aware of the trend of Icelandic politics, the situation assumed most startling possibilities for future complications of a very grave character.

"Firstly, Iceland needed money badly. Secondly, she had been watching closely for a quarter of a century the ever-Increasing inroads Norway was making by her constant encroachments seaward, thus pushing out the British trawler further and further into the deeper and less lucrative waters of the Atlantic. Against the British Government's stand for a three-mile the Norwegians opposed their four-mile demand, and whilst the British Government stoutly held to their three-mile claim, private instructions were issued from London to honour the four.

"Iceland noticed the Varanger Fjord fall into Oslo's rapacious maw with a 50-mile baseline, and gave a gasp when Norway insolently added four miles outside of the said baseline, thus even overshadowing Finnish territory. West Fjord followed suit with an 80-mile baseline, and then all fjords were closed. Then Iceland smiled when she saw her big brother go one better still.

"Norway then sent out her lusty scouts to scour the outside waters, and they came across some evidence of rock just showing at low water-mark when there was a heavy swell. To this God-sent far-flung sentinel of the deep, baselines were again projected from the mainland, and the usual capping of four miles added.

"Then to Iceland, after the above pantomime, was accorded the glorious transformation scene of our Government officials hurrying across the country pleading for special concentration areas being allowed further still, on behalf of that elusive phantom of Norwegian mythology, the starving fishermen of Norway; the area of the foregoing concentration grounds being but about one million acres of first-class fishing-ground.

"During the early part of the present year, the Althing at Reykjavik, Iceland, seriously discussed the violation of the North Sea Convention with its ten-mile baseline, and suggested the closing of the Faxa Fjord for a start, other bays to follow in due course. England was to be asked for a loan of £100,000 and excess quotas to be allowed of Icelandic fish into our country, to strike further blows at our already menaced fishing trade, thus following up the deadly attack of her Norwegian brother, who has been allowed to flood our inland markets directly with such deadly cutting competition within the last two years, with the very fish taken from grounds from which British vessels have been so summarily excluded. Be it remembered that it was stated quite seriously and fairly recently, in the Storthing, that Norway held similar immemorial rights over the whole of the North Sea, but she did not intend advancing the same at this present issue.

"Referring to the espionage and forwarding of patrol boat information as to whereabouts, the letter sent by me to the French Minister of Foreign Affairs at Paris practically explains the whole position. Copies of this letter were also transmitted to the various French firms interested, and I am gratified to see they have each given me loyal support, and maintained their agencies according to my request. Likewise, with the London tourist agency, a firm businesslike attitude was adopted by them in the same direction, and by the foregoing kindly help has thwarted a mean attack on the very livelihood and means of subsistence of a whole family, most of whose members were entirely unconcerned in the matter in dispute.

"Not content with instituting a vicious and one-sided prosecution for the simplest offence re patrol information, the Icelandic Government conspired, apart from the heavy fines which their Court intended and finally actually did impose, to pursue still further by wresting away all the agents' means of living, and all this to swell the finances of the Government by adding fresh agencies to their Tourist and Agency Bureau. The Zoegas were not in the slightest concerned or implicated in the serious charge of purloining the secret code-books belonging to the Ministry. The Government know who was the person responsible for the stealth, but for reasons known only to themselves, they refrain from prosecution.

"If reference be made to the remarks uttered by Mr. Larus Fjeldsted when conducting the case in Court at Reykjavik, in his summing-up for the defence, in them will be found tersely stated the main point of Mr. Zoega and the British trawler's defence in a very reasonable manner, and if the preamble to Bill 1928 be included, there is quite sufficient proof that Iceland was seriously aware of the breakage of the law by the Icelandic trawler and owner and took no steps whatever to rectify the same the Bill being vetoed for 16 sessions in the four years I 928 to 1932. However can Iceland justify its present action against British agents alone, for what is arguable even as a minor offence, and fail entirely to institute any inquiry whatever against their own nationals, after such insistent warnings and admissions in Parliament as disclosed?

"There can be but one answer, and that is Iceland is determined at any cost to hamper our industry, whilst providing every facility for its own.

"Its laws are not reliably applied, but used as a means of procuring, or rather extracting, foreign capital as occasion warrants. It was most certainly expected that the heavy fines and expenses (£3,000) imposed on the British Icelandic agents would be met by hard cash from England, and to their chagrin this has not fructified. Iceland, like Norway, is out for what she can get, and it is time that we in England woke up to the fact, and protected our interests.

"Surely the large trawler firms that have gone into liquidation during the last few years and the serious position of the industry as it stands, is sufficient indication to warrant instant consideration.

"I am afraid that most of these fishery disputes are too lightly dismissed, with the mistaken idea that fishing voyages are simply piratical conspiracies consisting of glorious infringements into the limits, deliberately carried out and crowned with ease and success. Occasional lapses of illegal fishing there may be, but they are only occasional.

"The fact remains that the bulk of your voyages out into these far-off waters are procured solely by straightforward, honest application, nights and days of unremitting toil, where sleep is practically unknown, and every minute of the operation is fraught with untold danger to life and limb, apart from the terrible weather conditions that so ruthlessly apply in these waters.

"Try and appreciate the worries and difficulties of every skipper under these conditions of toil, having to be ever watching his bearings, course and distances as his craft proceeds straining with her wires taut to breaking point, dragging the mass of doors and huge steel bobbins along the bottom, the vessel battered and shaken by every sea that rolls against her; the faint shore lights obscured by driving rain, mist or snow, heavy sea and wind drifts setting at defiance all exactness of dead reckoning. Then when day breaks, the same conditions, with most landmarks blotted out with a pall of cloud mist.

"Put the finest navigators under similar conditions, and what a mess they would make of it. The last case which came under my notice was on the above lines, and the patrol boat stayed twenty-four hours on the spot before he could procure what he considered reliable bearings.

"A fisherman cannot lie idle for twenty-four hours, he has to take the risks. Yet the Icelandic Court, with such an admission before them, failed to make any sympathetic allowance whatever, and imposed a very heavy fine.

"The Court lay mind fails to appreciate that the water immediately on the other side of the limit belongs to the fishermen, and in some cases he must fish close to the limits if he wishes to procure a certain catch at certain times of the year. So in every case the skipper is treated as an incorrigible rogue, fined and bullied, fish and gear confiscated, vessel delayed, in port during inquiry two to three days, and the best part of a month's work lost.

"Faced with the above conditions, is it such a serious offence if a skipper tries to find out the whereabouts of patrol boats, so that he is not haunted during his toil and stress by that watchful eye ever prying to see if he is making a false move, sometimes very close at hand during the night watches, with lights 'doused', or by day laid behind the nearest corner of land, unsympathetic, more than antagonistic?

"What applies to Iceland applies equally to Norwegian grounds. All trawlers fishing eastward of the North Cape have been pushed so far out seawards, that in many places the least deviation brings them within the law, and a trend outwards takes them over into an abyss, as they are now forced out close to the edge of the plateau, and one false move spells disaster.

"Personally, I think the time has come when the trade must take up a firm stand in the matter, and demand from the Foreign Office that a more humane attitude be adopted regarding fishing in these referred-to waters, otherwise all fish caught by either of these two nations should be denied entry into our country, and if the officials in London will not provide immediate redress, then the trade unions of workers should be approached, with a view towards their refusing to handle any consignments of fish landed at Newcastle, Grimsby, Hull, or other port in Great Britain.

"The present vindictive attack on British Icelandic agents should be strongly deprecated by our Foreign Office, and Iceland ordered to run its business on straight lines.

"It is very difficult for trade associations to interfere with the legal procedure of another country, but diplomatic channels can many times effect adjustments of abuses without unduly straining friendly relationships.

"Whilst I am afraid I may seem to have written very bitterly on the above matters, it is only the seriousness of the matters at issue that have compelled me, very unwillingly, to do so, seeing that I hold no animosity towards either country, as I have received many kindnesses during my frequent visits, and treasure the very many close friendships that have accrued thereby and trust sincerely to retain, both in Government circles, business and private."

·   ·   ·   ·   ·   ·

Mr. Smith has referred to a Bill brought before the Althing by an Icelandic Member, Mr. Svenn Olafsson. In introducing this Bill, the Member said: "Since the Icelandic trawlers commenced fishing operations in this country, it has been well known that some of them have fished a great deal in territorial waters. Moreover, since wireless stations were built and wireless apparatus installed in the trawlers, it has strongly been suspected that individual fishing concerns have directed illegal fishing from ashore. The Parliament records even contain a declaration from one of the oldest and most noteworthy fishing vessel-owners in Iceland, Mr. Ag. Flygenring, to this effect.

"It is known that some of the trawling companies in this country maintain a close espionage on every movement of the patrol ships and warn their ships, and that a trawler has on three consecutive days received telegrams here from Reykjavik reading thus: 'Grandmother is well. . . . Grandmother is still well. . . . Grandmother is beginning to be sick.' When the two former telegrams were sent, the patrol ship lay in harbour, but the third was sent as it was leaving the harbour. The purpose is obvious, that it is to inform Icelandic fishing vessels for a time they can with impunity rob the territorial waters. There are two dangers arising from the security afforded by wireless telegrams for Icelandic fishing vessels to violate the territorial waters.

"Foreign fishing vessels pursue the Icelandic ships into territorial waters, and escape with them. This has often been investigated and proved by the patrol ships. In the second place, in spite of commonly and accepted infringements, it is hardly ever possible to capture the Icelandic trawlers fishing in the territorial waters. This more than anything else will incline foreigners to mistrust Icelandic justice. Owners of foreign ships conclude that the laws are enforced principally against aliens, whilst the chief culprits escape unpunished in their own country.

"With this Bill the first step is taken in the direction of preventing the proved abuse of wireless telegrams in concealing violation of the territorial waters. Supervision abroad is common in such cases. Thus, for instance, the English wireless telegraphy authorities have discouraged Icelandic trawlers and the Icelandic Steamship Company's ships from their practice of having unnecessary and lengthy communication with the English coast, by listening to their conversation and sending to the Icelandic authorities copies of their telegrams, complaining of the conduct of the ships.

"It appears to be obviously a national necessity to prevent in future wireless telegrams from being misused for violation of the territorial waters.

•   •   •   •   •   •

The following letter, addressed by Mr. Smith to the French Minister of Foreign Affairs in Paris, throws
    further light on the subject.

Fish Docks,
Grimsby.
24th March 1936.
The Minister of Foreign Affairs, Paris,
France.

Dear Sir,

In the early part of this year our Ministry of Agriculture and Fisheries informed me that proceedings had been instituted against our agent at Reykjavik for supplying information to our vessels as to whereabouts of patrol ships and the office of the mentioned agent was being raided by the police.

I immediately took passage to Reykjavik so that I could make a full inquiry into the matter on the trade's behalf

Mr. Zoega's family have acted as our agents for fully 30 years and are well known to us personally, and hold an esteemed position in their business dealings at Reykjavik, therefore it was essential that I should accord every help and assistance in the above inquiry.

On my arrival I found the Court proceedings had been instituted, and the Government papers were very excited and abusive in their leaders and comments, and our agents were threatened with prison unless they made a full confession of their connivance.

This outburst was all directed against the agents of the British trawlers, as though they were the only offenders, and it would seem that this was the first time the Government had any knowledge that information was being received from the shore as to movements of patrol vessels. Now this was from the facts. The Icelandic Government, patrol vessels and Icelandic people have known fully well that, for the last 25 years, trawlers have been receiving messages, and the Government took no steps whatever to make the slightest inquiries into the matter, or try to stop the practice. Now during the whole of the 25 years Icelandic trawlers have used shore agencies for information, and this factor accounted For the many successful voyages of fish which these purely Icelandic owned vessels were able to land in England, France, and Germany. It is only within the last three years that any British trawlers took advantage of the Icelandic shore agencies re patrol boats, and I very much doubt whether it could be shown that more than four companies out of our many firms received any information at all.

Seeing the authorities had allowed their own vessels to violate their laws with impunity for 25 years, it seemed to me very unfair that British vessels should be credited solely with the whole offence and our agent victimized. I placed my views strongly in interview before their Minister, and requested that he should put a stop to this one-sided inquiry and unjust and very objectionable publicity.

I obtained no definite promises from the Minister, but from that date, until the present, all proceedings have been stayed, and I was hoping that we should hear nothing further.

There have not been any inquiries whatever made against a single Icelandic owned trawler at Reykjavik. This speaks for itself. The boats are owned by Members of the Government, and it was never intended to prosecute Icelandic owners.

I pointed out to their Minister that we as a trade would give them every support in enforcing the law, but it was essential that the law must be administered impartially, and against every offender.

I finally requested that no vindictive measures or reprisals should be taken against the agents concerned, seeing they were but the servants of the trawler owners and acting under owners' instructions. Unfortunately for our agents, the Icelandic Government have instituted a Government Tourist Travel Bureau, and Agency Bureau for Iceland, and it is essential they should have some clients to make it a paying concern. The present was considered an opportune time to enrich themselves at the expense of the Zoegas, who were in possession of some very important agencies.

Icelandic politics are not too clean, but this victimization of the Zoegas is liable to go too far.

We were able to oppose their designs in England, but rumour has it that the Icelandic Government have enlisted the services of the French Vice-Consul at Reykjavik to interfere and divert, if possible, the French agencies from the Zoegas. If this be so (which I sincerely hope it is not) it means that the French Consulate is being used very unworthily to punish and stigmatize a gentleman of unquestionable business standing.

Surely the Vice-Consul must recognize that his interest lies more with the trawling industry of foreigners than it does with the interests of Iceland. When I attended at Iceland I considered that I was looking after the interests of all foreign vessels, when I took the stand I did, but it is very disturbing to find that whilst the Icelandic Government and Court suspended judgment on the agents, the French Consul steps in and judges and punishes. If he will look into the records at his office in Reykjavik, he will find there a dossier relating to a French vessel the *La Provence*. This vessel was caught for illegal fishing and fined, her fish confiscated and also her gear. After a lengthy appeal she won her case and got back the fine, but I very much doubt if she has yet recovered her claim for the loss she sustained by the forced sale of her fish at Iceland.

After reading about the La Provence, the Consul will perhaps sympathize a little with, and understand why, the trawler skippers try to find out where the patrol boat is. A trawler does not want to know where the patrol boat is because he wishes to fish within the limits. It is quite possible the trawler's skipper wishes to know where the patrol boat is, so that if the patrol boat be anywhere near, the trawler will then keep a full mile off the limit for fear that the patrol skipper will make a slight mistake in his bearings, and make a false accusation, as was done in the case of the La Provence, which resulted in a loss to the French owners of thousands of pounds sterling. If the Consul will peruse the La Provence case I think he will modify his views, and see some justice on the trawlers' side, and that it is necessary certainly at the present not to trust to much to the tender mercies of the patrol. We have a case similar to the La Provence; it is also unsettled so far as recovery of our claim for loss of fish against the Icelandic Government, and there are many other of a like nature pending settlement. We, as you will appreciate from our heading, are concerned with insurance matters purely and simply, and have no connection with the fishing side of the trade or its finances but we are perturbed at the serious increase of fines impose very arbitrarily on vessels in Icelandic waters. A fine of £1,000 has been inflicted this year for faulty stowage of gear, and it is necessary there should be some co-operation of interests in connection with this matter among foreign owner otherwise we shall be gradually forced away from legitimate grounds in the Icelandic vicinity. Iceland is well able look after her own interests without outside help, seeing all the inquiries are conducted in her own courts at Iceland where prejudice runs very high, and there is a serious bias favour of the evidence of the patrol.

We would respectfully ask from you that no steps taken at such a critical time as the present to play into the hands of the Icelanders, as by doing so it will only add the many difficulties which we are labouring under, and impose further burdens on our trawler skippers in wresting a precarious living in these northern waters.

I am convinced that the whole dispute is mixed up with political propaganda, and the Socialist Government of Iceland is merely taking the present opportunity of attacking the opposition party (Conservative) through its members. This is quite evident from the fact that no Government trawler owner or concern has suffered the slightest in this attack. Seeing such publicity has been given and warnings issued, it would be hopeless now to demand or investigate inquiries, as by this time all incriminating documents will have been destroyed.

Had the Government initially searched all Icelandic trawlers for documents and codes, within her own ports, they would have procured all the evidence they required; but this was not their wish, and we are faced with the fact that absolutely no inquiry has been prosecuted against their own vessels within their own jurisdiction up to the present.

We, like yourselves, in no wise sympathize with the obtaining of information from the shore as to the movements of patrols, and are doing all we can to stop such practice for the future, but we must insist, in common fairness, that prosecutions made by the Icelandic Government shall be impartially made against not only foreigners, but equally against their own vessels in future.

If we can be fully assured of the foregoing, we as a trade will accord them our most earnest support in honouring their laws.

This letter is written somewhat in haste, and I must apologize for its undue length, but I can assure you that the matter dealt with is worthy of your earnest attention, and we as British owners would consider it an act of grace were your office to kindly withhold judgment or action against agents referred to; at least it would be only fair to wait until legal judgment has been declared, seeing such judgment has not been given up to the present.

If I am wrong in presuming that your office had intention of acting to the detriment of the Zoega firm, I humbly apologize for my error, but I still request your good offices and co-operation in compelling Icelandic authority to conform to equitable procedure in dealing with foreign trawlers in general.

Believe me to remain,
Respectfully yours,
J. Smith,
Secretary.

. . . . . .

Not long ago a rather curious incident occurred which, in the minds of some in Grimsby, was merely an effort to whitewash the Icelandic Government.

Two Icelandic trawlers put into Grimsby, and the Vice-Consul here intimated the desire of the Reykjavik police that the Grimsby police should search the vessels for codes or other material that might furnish evidence of alleged complicity in fish poaching.

Later the Vice-Consul Wrote an article to the Press in which he declared that the Government investigations were concerned with all trawlers fishing in Icelandic waters, irrespective of nationality.

He went on to refer to the fact that the Grimsby police had been requested to search two Icelandic trawlers on their arrival here, with the result that certain documents were forwarded to Iceland.

Mr. Smith describes this as a put-up job by the Icelandic Government to hoodwink the British Foreign Office.

"Why should the Grimsby Police be handed the invidious task of undertaking such inquiry as above? These vessels had sailed from Iceland, and if suspicion had been aroused as to their method of carrying out their fishing, why did not the Icelandic police take over their own dirty work? The proper and, I think I am right in stressing, the surest way would have been to have raided the vessels and also the offices on shore at Reykjavik itself.

"Why allow the skippers and owners concerned to have all that time in which to get rid of evidence during the passage to Grimsby; when they could have acted suddenly with hope of some success?

"The truth must be that no incriminating documents were found whatever, which is quite natural to suppose, and the two vessels were used as decoys in the political game at issue, which is to cover up their enmity against British fishing interests, as has been clearly indicated for years.

"We assert that Iceland has not instituted one single inquiry or prosecution against any of her own nationals."

Chapter 10

THE HARVEST

Aboard S.T. Arsenal.
Homeward Bound.

D uring several months of the year, particularly from January to June, large catches of fish, chiefly cod, are landed from the White Sea and Bear Island, and prices slump to such an extent that tons of fish are sent to the manure dump. The quantity sold often realizes less than ten pence per stone, which means that each vessel is unable to clear expenses, resulting in the Skipper and Mate settling in debt.

This happens trip after trip during this season, and we simple fishermen are told that the inexorable law of supply and demand is the sole and only explanation. The middlemen will not purchase a greater quantity of fish than they require for their retail customers, and their demand seldom varies, but could not something be done with the huge quantities of fish which are sent with ruthless and unfailing regularity to the manure pits? This fish could be salted or even cured, as they are now doing in Norway, and would keep indefinitely.

It is a well-known fact that, as far as food is concerned, we are not a self-supporting nation, and the time may come when an adequate supply of food stores may be equally, if not more important, than an immense *Arsenal* of aeroplanes, guns, battleships, and shells.

Two years ago, on 25th November, I left Grimsby for Bear Island, 75 North. I reckoned the trip would take me about twenty-five days, which would give me ample time to get back for my daughter's wedding day, which had been fixed to take place on Christmas Eve.

Every day of the outward voyage we battled against nor'-easterly gales, and I had to constantly ease the engines down to avoid damage to both the ship and gear. The weather continued during the whole of the fishing operations, and in between towing I was constantly at the wheel, keeping her head to wind, to prevent the seas from sweeping us to hell.

For fourteen days we struggled on, in blizzard and fog, the men wet to the skin every haul. The temperature dropped to 40 below, and in between shooting and mending, hauling and gutting, the brats were incessantly employed chopping ice from the riggings and sides of the ship to keep her from becoming top-heavy and capsizing. During the whole of this time we averaged less than an hour's sleep each day.

Try and imagine the conditions the men had to face in the fish-pounds under these conditions, exposed eternally on the lurching, sea-swept decks. But we were happy, happy, because with each haul the swag-bag came up full to bursting-point…prime, hard sprags.

I turned her nose, homeward bound, and had just seven days to reach Grimsby before my little girl was due to leave the old home nest.

"We'll just do it nicely," I said to Paddy, my Chief Engineer; "give her all she's got."

Then I turned in for a spell, handing over to Abe, my Mate.

God disposes! Before I had got my old crust on the feathers I was called to the bridge again, and there I remained without a break until we crawled through the lock-pits…two days late; but only by the grace of God did we reach there at all. Incessant gales lashed us every inch of the way, dread mountains of foaming green seas rose to meet us at every yard.

One dread, tremendous sea leaped up, and crashed, with the force of an eighty-mile gale behind it, on to the wheelhouse. I felt the vessel shudder from the awful driving force of that savage water. She heeled to port, with the funnel literally flat on the waters. I heard the rending of steel, and the crashing of loosened gear, and shut my eyes praying.

For the first time in my life my mind dwelt on the possibility of sinking. But up she came again, shaking her battered head, snorting contempt.

"Good girl . . . good old *Arsenal* . . . up and over, lass, up and over!"

Yes, I praised her aloud, and blessed the wisdom of her builders.

Down below, watching the big-ends thunder their cycles, oil-can in hand, eyes glued on pressure gauges, Paddy played his gallant part, nursing, easing, driving, sometimes almost standing on his head.

Near him, gravely watching, sat Minnie, the cat, and near her, Blackie, blinking encouragement to their great-hearted friend.

"What's she doing, Paddy?"

"One hundred and forty, Skipper... all she's got!"

One hundred and forty revolutions to the minute, and against the terrific wind and sea we were barely making three knots.

Every window on the bridge was boarded up. My eyes peered ahead, through little peep-holes barely an inch in diameter; but even these were useless. We were driving blind, visibility nil, and thus we steamed for six days and nights.

Dimly through the peepholes, obscured eternally by lashing spray, the dread grandeur of the endless breakers held me petrified. One minute perched on a mighty crest, rolling, shuddering, the next hurtling down into a bottomless pit. Then on again, climbing a mountainous wall of churning green.

The days passed, and Charlie, the cook, reported that our provisions were almost finished. Next, Paddy informed me that he had reached the last bunker of coal. But God was with us. Three days before Christmas the wind eased, the seas abated, and we limped into the shelter of Stromness, feeling that at last we were safe.

There we obtained food and coal, and sent our messages to the waiting women at home.

Another trawler, the St. Merryn, a Yorkie, had crawled into Stromness, also short of food and coal, and we sailed out side by side to face the last few miles of 'Hell's Gates'-the dreaded Pentland Firth.

Reaching the North Sea, another gale sprang up, and through the gloom, as darkness fell, we saw the other trawler turn back. The Skipper of the St. Merryn, old and experienced, knew the limit of his ship.

"I advise you to turn back, Albert," he wirelessed. "I can smell more wind ahead."

For a moment I was tempted, but we had been absent for twenty-nine days, and my fish were not improving, so I decided to carry on.

A few hours later that night a quiet voice reached me over the air. It came from the Skipper of the trawler *Amethyst*, homeward bound from the White Sea.

"Hello, Albert. We have just shipped a tremendous sea-Chief Engineer reports boiler has shifted about two inches from its bed plate. I'm afraid it's the end, old man. . . . Can you reach us?"

We were not many miles away, but barely making five knots, and only one more message reached us from the helpless vessel.

"Good-bye, Albert. . . . Au revoir!"

But why stress the tragedy of that one voyage, no uncommon experience in this eternal gamble. All too often we prance up the broad waters of the Humber, licking the scars of a hundred battles, the brats wearied to the point of physical and mental exhaustion, too tired even to sleep, but happy in the thought that the ice-pounds under the for'ard hatches are crammed with loot...hard sprags, ducks, and jumbos, greeneyes, coalies, skate, and flats...fine, prime fish fresh as on the day it was caught, only to see the relentless hammer of the auctioneer knock down sometimes less than half of the catch at a farthing a pound, and the greater part, tons of it, lying in unwanted heaps on the pontoon consigned to the manure heap.

On that eventful voyage, which I have just described, I landed 3,000 boxes of prime fish…and stood by whilst it was knocked down for 2s 6d a box. Eight stone of the finest quality Iceland cod for thirty pence.

I know there are many arguments. The law of supply and demand is the general cry, but surely the surplus, if there is a surplus, deserves a better fate than the manure heap. As I have written before, fish can be salted or canned and will keep for ever, They are even canning white fish in Norway now, cod and haddocks, and sending thousands of tons to our own British Dominions where they can't get this delicacy in their own waters. Again, we fishermen never hear of the public benefiting when round fish is being sold at an average of not more than twopence a pound all the year round, and generally considerably less.

If the poor people were to benefit sometimes we wouldn't mind so much. And when the greater part of our catch is relentlessly and ruthlessly thrown on the dung-heap every man of the crew suffers.

All the arguments and explanations in the world won't feed empty tummies, or allay the bitterness which we feel sometimes when, at the end of three weeks of heart-breaking, ceaseless toil we hear the parrot cry of the middleman . . . Glut!

Aye, it's not easy to stand helplessly by and witness prime food, sent us by the grace of God, consigned to the manure heap. That's something which we fishermen will never be able to understand, and all the business brains in the world will never be able to explain it to our satisfaction.

But with that off my chest my yarn is finished. The lights of the lock-pits are dead ahead.

The harbour lights beyond.

Home!

THE END

Chapter 11

THE WRECK OF THE *HOWE*

Note: The part played by Ernest Drinkall, Skipper of the Grimsby Trawler *ELF KING*, following the wreck of the *HOWE* on Bear Island, November 19th, 1931, in which no less than 30 other trawlers battled for three days in a desperate effort to save the stricken crew, is proclaimed by all fishermen as the bravest deed ever consummated in the Northern Seas.

One night on the rocks off Bear Island
A trawler named the *HOWE* ran ashore.
Right on those cursed hidden "blinders",
To remain there a wreck for ever more.
No tugs in the world could have saved her
But one went his luck there to try
And found her a wreck that was hopeless,
To leave her laid there, high and dry.

Her Skipper was a man named McGregor,
As brave as the brave known to be,
He said: "Now she's a wreck, boys, for ever,
But you'll still take your orders from me.
Your lives all depend on good discipline,
So be cheerful and keep a big heart.
For the sake of your wives and your families
Each of you must play your part."

But out in that dark Arctic region
Just imagine the dire plight of the crew,
With their ship on the rocks of Bear Island
There was nothing on earth they could do.
Their "Sparks" was a brave lad of twenty,

His message for help he had sent.
Thank God it was answered by plenty,
And bravely to her aid they went.

They found her a wreck at the mercy
Of a sea that no pen can describe.
They couldn't get anywhere near her
Yet times out of number they tried.
On the deck they could see the poor fellows standing,
And who would deny they were brave,
Facing their death, calm and steadfast,
On the brink of a sailor's grave

So round to the lee of the Island,
Each vessel sent picked men ashore
To battle across lad that was barren
And untrodden by human foot before.
And God only knows of that hardships,
They faced on that bleak winter night,
Hands, faces, feet were frost-bitten
But they struggled on without sup or bite.

On the *HOWE*, to that brave seaman, Harper,
A rope round his body they tied,
To swim to a point that meant rescue.
He failed, but I praise him, he tried.
He was pulled back on board by his comrades,
And there on that wreck he lay "beat",
The whitest of men you could meet.

Still high on those rocks up above them,
With courage, those men struggled on,
Till they found them, and brought off the rescue,
They saved the whole crew, everyone.
These lads were brought back to Grimsby,
And to see them again – it was grand!
We know not one half what they suffered,
But we kid them that we understand.

We thank you, brave men, for that rescue,
Your deed was truly gallant – well done!
It may not have gone down to history,

It is even forgotten by some.
But I myself, a fisherman –
Will remember to my dying day,
And no gold in the world can repay you,
Had they called it a job for pay.

And a word for you that were rescued,
For some of you are well known to me.
No words could I write that could praise you enough,
For your conduct, so gallant at sea.
You held up that fine British tradition,
You sent up its practice, sky high,
Those grim nights on the rocks at Bear Island,
Where in silence you were prepared to die.

Well, that is the life of the fisher
As told in this tale of the sea,
Lives are so often the price
Of that fish you have eaten for tea.
But seldom you'll hear those men grumble,
It's come day, or go day with them.
Just trusting to God in his mercy,
And thank Him for that – Amen!

    Albert Hutchinson